FORGOTTEN FOUNDER, DRUNKEN PROPHET

LIVES OF THE FOUNDERS

—————————————

EDITED BY JOSIAH BUNTING III

FORGOTTEN FOUNDER, DRUNKEN PROPHET

The Life of Luther Martin

Bill Kauffman

ISI
BOOKS

Wilmington, Delaware

Kauffman, Bill, 1959–

    Forgotten founder, drunken prophet : the life of Luther Martin / Bill
Kauffman.—1st ed.—Wilmington, Del. : ISI Books, c2008.

        p. ; cm.
        (Lives of the founders)

        ISBN: 978-1-61017-148-9
        Includes bibliographical references and index.

        1. Martin, Luther, 1748–1826. 2. United States—Politics and
government—1783–1789. 3. Constitutional history—United States.
4. United States. Constitutional Convention (1787)—History. I. Title.
II. Life of Luther Martin.

E302.6.M425 K38 2008   2008928223
973.4/092—dc22   0808

ISI Books
Intercollegiate Studies Institute
3901 Centerville Road
Wilmington, DE 19807-1938
www.isibooks.org

Manufactured in the United States of America

To the staff—past, present, and future—
of the Richmond Memorial Library,
cultural heart of my beloved Batavia

CONTENTS

CONTENTS

ACKNOWLEDGMENTS

———————

IN THE COURSE OF A RAMBLING (IF SPENT LARGELY IN ONE place) life I have found beer to be inspiration, and none more so than Jeremy Beer, editor in chief of ISI Books. Jeremy invited me to tell the story of my favorite Anti-Federalist, Luther Martin, and I toast him for it.

I honed, rather than hoved, I hope, part of this argument in a speech at Tufts University. Thanks to Chad Kifer, a fine man with an unaccountable passion for the Miami Dolphins, for setting that up.

The late William H. Riker, gentleman, scholar, and Federalist, sparked my interest in the Philadelphia convention during my malisoned graduate school pit stop almost twenty-five years ago. Thank you, Professor Riker. Sorry for dissing Madison.

Many thanks to Katie Papas and Brenda Reeb of Rush Rhees Library at the University of Rochester, who good-naturedly helped this techno-idiot use, if not understand, machines far beyond my comprehension. Thanks, too, to the staff of the Maryland Historical Society Library, whose archives contained several gems. I am again indebted to Paula Meyer of the Richmond Memorial Library for hunting down elusive books.

Finally, and firstly, this book does not exist without my family. I am forever grateful for the mysteries.

THE PEOPLE WHO LOST

"SO LET US THINK ABOUT THE PEOPLE WHO LOST," WROTE THE historian William Appleman Williams, who did not mean by that the 1925 Rochester Jeffersons but rather those unloved, perhaps unlovable, certainly defenderless, conservative presidents John Quincy Adams and Herbert Hoover, whose reclamation the left-wing Iowa patriot Williams undertook.[1]

We have a nasty habit of flushing down the memory hole "the people who lost." Or demonizing them. Going back in time and painting Snidely Whiplash mustaches on their luckless countenances.

Historians have not, on the whole, been kind to the Anti-Federalists, the misleading name slapped on those who opposed ratification of the Constitution. In the main—but not by Main, as we shall see—they have been written off as bucolic bumpkins unable to grasp the exquisiteness of the Madisonian argument or as agrarian radicals motivated by antipathy toward wealth, commerce, and table manners. They are sometimes, grudgingly, with many qualifications, given credit for siring, indirectly, the Bill of Rights, but more often they are swept aside as beetle-browed brutes incapable of appreciating the majesty of the Constitution or, as the old canard goes, as rural debtors fearful that the new Constitution would prevent states from issuing worthless paper money with which they could discharge the debts they had so imprudently run up. Well, hell, I'm a rural debtor myself, so permit me to say a few words for the Anti-Federalists: the original "people who lost."

"Men of little faith," the historian Cecelia M. Kenyon called them. Faith, that is, in the ability of other men to design a tentacular government that would come to cover the better part of a continent. "The Antifederalists reflected a relatively early stage in the evolution of modern republican thought," asseverated Kenyon, who conceded that while their ideas were "less advanced than those of the Federalists," they were "not uninteresting."[2] Cheapjack praise indeed. I'm not sure why an author would undertake a book on a subject for which she can muster no praise more lavish than that it is "not uninteresting."

The history of weights and measures is "not uninteresting." The jurisprudence of Sandra Day O'Connor is, maybe, if we're in a really generous mood, "not uninteresting." The radical and rooted objections of early American patriots to the Constitution are, I venture to say, downright interesting.

The Antis are the men—and women, I add, not as a P.C. genuflection but in recognition of the Bay State's Mercy Otis Warren, playwright and historian and among the most literary Anti-

Federalists—who considered what the delegates to the Constitutional Convention had wrought in that sweltering Philadelphia summer of 1787 and said No. They included dissenting delegates to that convention, like George Mason of Virginia; patriots still afire with the spirit of '76, like Patrick Henry; and backcountry farmers and cobblers and libertarian editors and malcontent layabouts. They were "not simply blockheads standing in the way of progress," wrote Robert Rutland in *The Ordeal of the Constitution*, "but . . . serious, oftentimes brilliant, citizens who viewed the Constitution in 1787–88 with something less than awe."[3]

The Anti-Federalists regarded consolidation of governmental power with what seems to me a meet suspicion, though it has seemed to others to verge on paranoia. One of my favorite Anti-Fed pseudonyms was taken by the writer who called himself "None of the Well-Born Conspirators."

They often made wild predictions about where this all would lead. For instance, George Clinton—not the funky parliamentarian but the New York Anti-Federalist—prophesied that the federal city created by the Constitution, later known as Washington, D.C., "would be the asylum of the base, idle, avaricious and ambitious."[4] Gee, thank God that never happened.

The Anti-Federalists raised a central question of political philosophy: Where ought political power to reside? In a remote central authority, or hard by the people? (My invidious phrasing, I admit.) A prominent Federalist—which is to say, using the down-is-up nomenclature devised by those crafty consolidationists, an advocate of the new Constitution—lectured that "we must forget our local habits and attachments,"[5] but this is only possible for those who *have* no local habits or attachments. One might as well enjoin that "we must forget our heart and lungs."

The sheer scope of this new system, the audacity of bringing thirteen far-flung states under one central government, astonished the Anti-Federalists. James Winthrop of Massachusetts marveled, "The idea of an uncompounded republick, on an average one thousand miles in length, and eight hundred in breadth, and containing six millions of white inhabitants all reduced to the same standard of morals, of habits, and of laws, is in itself an absurdity, and contrary to the whole experience of mankind. . . . Large and consolidated empires may indeed dazzle the eyes of a distant spectator with their splendour, but if examined more nearly are always found to be full of misery."[6]

More poetically, a Charleston versifier lamented:

Ye, who have bled in Freedom's sacred cause,
Ah, why desert her maxims and her laws?
   When *thirteen* states are moulded into *one*
Your rights are vanish'd and your honors gone;
The form of Freedom alone shall remain,
As Rome had Senators when she hugg'd the chain.[7]

The Antis were not quibblers, not captious carpers arguing about dotted i's and uncrossed t's. Their objections cut to the heart of the new Constitution. Indeed, they began with the preamble. Samuel Adams, brewer and sometime Anti-Federalist, upon reading "We the People of the United States," remarked wryly, "as I enter the Building I stumble at the Threshold. I meet with a National Government, instead of a Federal Union of Sovereign States."[8] Patrick Henry stumbled, too: "The question turns, sir, on that poor little thing—the expression, We, the people, instead of the states, of America"—a locution that was "extremely pernicious, impolitic, and dangerous."[9]

While the Federalists admired the finely wrought constitutional machinery, with its balance of powers, its cunning methods of nullifying the harmful effects of faction, of cupidity, of powerlust, the Anti-Federalists struck at the root. "For the Anti-Federalists," wrote the historian Herbert J. Storing, "government is seen as itself the major problem."[10]

They objected to almost every feature of the Constitution. Anti-Federalists wanted annual elections. A larger House of Representatives whose members were paid by the states, not the central government, so that they did not forget on which side their bread was buttered. Rotation in office, or term limits. A Bill of Rights. Limitations on standing armies. No "general welfare" clause, which, as the Biddeford, Massachusetts, Anti-Federalist Silas Lee predicted, would "be construed to extend to every matter of legislation."[11]

At the head of this unitary state was a single executive whose powers were insufficiently checked. "Who can deny," asked "Philadelphiensis," that "the *president general* will be . . . a king elected to command a standing army?"[12]

The Anti-Federalists stood for decentralism, local democracy, antimilitarism, and a deep suspicion of central governments. And they stood on what they stood for. Local attachments. Local knowledge. While the Pennsylvania Federalist Gouverneur Morris "flattered himself he came here in some degree as a Representative of the whole human race,"[13] Anti-Federalists understood that one cannot love an abstraction such as "the whole human race." One loves particular flesh-and-blood members of that race. "My love must be discriminate / or fail to bear its weight,"[14] in the words of a modern Anti-Federalist, the Kentucky poet-farmer Wendell Berry. He who loves the whole human race seldom has much time for individual members thereof.

Contra the court historians, the Antis were cautious, prudent, grounded, attached. They were not the party of vainglory in 1787–88. "Under no circumstances did Antifederalists think of themselves as immortals winning undying fame for themselves," wrote Michael Lienesch. "In fact, they were at their rhetorical best in scoffing at the pretentions [sic] of those Federalists who pictured themselves in the role of classical legislators."[15]

They were plain people whose homely dreams ran not to national greatness. What to men of station was the periphery was to them the heart. Massachusetts Anti Amos Singletary of Worcester County told the state's ratifying convention that "These lawyers and men of learning, and moneyed men that talk so finely, and gloss over matters so smoothly, to make us, poor illiterate people, swallow down the pill, expect to get into Congress themselves; they expect to be the managers of this Constitution, and get all the power and all the money into their own hands, and then they will swallow up all us little folks . . . just as the whale swallowed up Jonah."[16]

Things were spiralling out of control. The scale was getting too big. Anti-Federalist Samuel Chase of Maryland (whose path we will cross again) objected that "the distance between the people and their Representatives will be so very great that there is no probability of a Farmer or Planter being chosen. Mechanics of every Branch will be excluded by a general voice from a Seat. Only the Gentry, the Rich & well born will be elected."[17]

This seems to me incontrovertibly true, and never more so than today. In smaller polities representatives are, in some sense, representative. My town council includes an electrician, a housewife, a custodian, and my lovely wife, whose academic training was in philosophy. This, I daresay, is a far more representative body than the U.S. Congress, and the town council's nearness to its constituency endows it with a legitimacy. I may not always agree with its acts but I can remonstrate, face to face, with those who make the local laws. I cannot do so at the national level. And our town council, whatever mistakes it might make, does not have blood dripping from its claws.

This exordium leads us, finally, to my subject, the Anti's Anti, the man who is, without doubt, the least honored delegate to the Constitutional Convention.

Martin Luther launched a reformation. Martin Luther King Jr. got a national holiday. Yet what does their nominal inversion, Luther Martin, get? No respect. The total eclipse of this unfortunate son was observed as early as January 1869, when the *Saturday Bulletin* noted of Martin: "He has only been dead about forty years, and yet his name has almost passed into oblivion. . . . As it is, his fame is mainly traditionary, and in another generation will be almost forgotten."[18] In 1903, after recounting Martin's eventful life, Ashley M. Gould told the Maryland State Bar Association, "No monuments are erected to do reverence to his memory; there is no published edition of his works."[19]

I am no account as a monument builder but among my venial sins I am a novelist, and I've wondered for nigh unto twenty-five years now why no one has written a novelistic treatment of Luther Martin's life.

He was . . . well, let's take a look at his press clippings.

William Pierce, the Georgia delegate who left us capsule sketches of his fellow immortals, wrote of Martin that "This Gentleman possesses a good deal of information, but he has a very bad delivery, and so extremely prolix, that he never speaks without tiring the patience of all who hear him."[20]

Chief Justice Roger Taney remembered Martin's "utter disregard of good taste and refinement in his dress and language and . . . manner of eating."[21] (Aha, says my wife, the long-suffering Lucine, who has identified me as a housemartin.)

A New Jersey farmboy of modest origins, a top scholar at the College of New Jersey (later Princeton), a teacher in Maryland, a young lawyer on the make, Luther Martin's humble origins and eccentric behavior left him "a misfit in the Maryland aristocracy," as Forrest McDonald writes.[22]

Popular accounts of the Constitutional Convention designate Martin as the villain—think a circa-1973 hybrid of Dennis Hopper and Ernest Borgnine, endlessly talkative but fitfully coherent, an obstructionist, a naysayer. He is the town drunk, the class bore, the motormouth. Though at Princeton he had been active in the Well Meaning Society, a debate club, this seems to have affected him rather as the Catholic catechism did young Ted Kennedy. It didn't take. Martin tried well meaning, found it wanting, and lit out for Verbosity Hill.

Historians have not been kind to Luther Martin. "He proved to be a tiresome speaker,"[23] says Max Farrand, who ascribes this fault to Martin's "school-teaching days."[24] To Clinton Rossiter he is "garrulous, sour, and pigheaded," albeit "an influential pricker of egos and consciences."[25] Catherine Drinker Bowen refers to "his boisterous and interminable harangues"; Martin, as she describes him in Philadelphia, "was about forty, broad of shoulder, carelessly dressed, with short hair, a long nose, a rough voice and a convivial liking for the bottle which later was to lead him into insolvency and disgrace. He was impulsive, undisciplined, altogether the wild man of the Convention, furious defender of state sovereignty, by no means foolish in all he said."[26]

In any event, Martin is glimpsed through a shot glass, darkly. The imagery of alcohol, of dipsomania, surrounds him, imbibes him. Brandy—what a good wife she would be. Martin never denied his habitual intoxication but offered only this exculpatory remark: "In the heat of the summer my health requires that I should drink in abundance to supply the amazing waste from perspiration."[27] The sweat defense.

His villainy extends even into Jean Fritz's popular children's book, *Shh! We're Writing the Constitution* (1987). Her Martin is "a tall, mussed-up looking man who loved the sound of his own voice so much that once he started talking, he couldn't bear to stop. He . . . was so boring that Madison didn't even bother to write it all down and Benjamin Franklin went to sleep."[28] Well, look: Franklin would have fallen asleep during a lap dance, and Madison was a selective, not to mention tendentious, secretary. Jean Fritz also accuses Martin of swiping books from the Philadelphia library. I suppose that only a word-count-conscious editor kept her from indicting poor Luther for chewing gum in class and running in the halls.

Yet scratch hard enough and the tarnish of eleven score years fades to reveal another Martin. He was also, as the historian M. E. Bradford has written, "The tireless champion of the sovereignty of the states . . . A cheerful pessimist . . . and a great original."[29] His eristic talents were widely celebrated. Chief Justice William H. Rehnquist called Martin "one of the great lawyers in American history, and also one of the great iconoclasts of the American legal profession."[30] In his marvelous novel *Burr* (1973), Gore Vidal's narrator describes his hero's attorney as "the redoubtable Tory, the drunk, the brilliant, the incomparable Luther Martin (easily the best trial lawyer of our time)."[31]

"The federalistic principles found in the Constitution are largely a result of concessions to [Martin's] demands," wrote historian Everett D. Obrecht. "Without his presence in the convention, the new national government would have been far more powerful."[32] Yet it was still too powerful for Luther Martin. He left Philadelphia on September 4, 1787, and though he did not return to give "my solemn negative" to the document, he did phone in a request, as it were: "that as long as the history of mankind shall record the appointment of the late Convention, and the system which has been proposed by them, it is my highest ambition that my name also be recorded as one who considered the system injurious to my country, and as such opposed it."[33]

Consider it done, Luther.

Let us revisit the Philadelphia experiment. . . .

PART ONE

THE PHILADELPHIA STORY

THE MOST TEDIOUS SECTION OF ANY BIOGRAPHY OF A FOUND-ing Father—or Confounding Father, as per Luther Martin—is that three- or four-page stretch of genealogy that we impatiently browse to get to the good stuff. I am tempted to follow Elmore Leonard's sage advice to novelists to *"leave out all the parts readers skip,"*[1] especially given the paucity of extant information on "all that David Copperfield" stuff about Luther Martin.

But let me instead recommend the only biography of Martin ever published—*Luther Martin of Maryland* (1970) by Paul S. Clarkson and R. Samuel Jett.[2] Coauthor Clarkson was a book collector, Sherlock Holmesian, highly decorated Baker Street Irregular, and founder of the Six Napoleons of Baltimore. Clarkson and Jett did an uncommonly fine job filling in the details of Martin's legal career. Theirs was a labor of Maryland piety and of love.

What little we know of Luther Martin's early life comes from the horse's disputatious mouth, for Martin left an autobiographical fragment in the form of a curious five-part pamphlet titled *Modern Gratitude* (1802).

Invective-filled, freeswinging, written at white heat and white hate and directed at the cad who seduced his fifteen-year-old daughter, *Modern Gratitude* is the source of most of our knowledge of Martin's life before his Philadelphia summer. Rather like a blog, it lacked an editorial filter, and so the foulest calumnies are hurled at Richard Raynal Keene, the Baltimore Lothario who insinuated himself into Martin's home and stole dear Eleonora. Daddy, as was his wont, came out swinging. But more on that anon.

"I am an American born, of the fourth or fifth generation," declared Martin, lest anyone suspect from his periodic uncouthness that he was fresh off the boat. His forbears had come to the new world from the west of England as early as 1623 and settled in the Piscataqua region of what is now New Hampshire. Clarkson and Jett fix as the fall of 1666 the migration of the leading families of Piscataqua to an area east of New Brunswick, New Jersey, near the Raritan River. The settlers named their new place Piscataqua, after that which they had left. It was "an uncultivated wilderness," Martin reminds us, "inhabited by its copper-coloured aborigines."[3] Today it is Piscataway, best known as home of the Rutgers Scarlet Knights.

"My ancestors were, and most of their descendants have been, of that class or 'sect' of people known as agriculturalists or cultivators of the earth," writes Martin, who cannot record even such boilerplate without setting aside a clause in which he sneers at the hated "sage philosopher" Thomas Jefferson's estimation that such are "God's chosen people."[4] Why did he detest Jefferson, the Founding deity nighest unto the Anti-Federalist persuasion? Patience, dear reader. No shortcuts via the index, please.

Martin's birth year is variously dated at 1744 and 1748, though by his own account the latter date seems accurate. Clarkson and Jett, the most trustworthy of later sources, estimate his day of birth at February 20, 1748. He was the third of nine children borne by Hannah Martin of her husband Benjamin. All lived to maturity—a rare nonuple.

In August of his thirteenth year, young man Luther "was sent to Princeton college,"[5] then known as the College of New Jersey, seedbed of the Constitutional Convention. His college chums included a fellow New Jerseyan, William Paterson, who proposed the true federalist alternative in Philadelphia in 1787, and thus is the father of the constitutional republic of the America that never happened.

Of the thirty-one (Martin says thirty-five) members of his Princeton class of 1766, Martin ranked first in languages and, by his own account, *second to none* in the *sciences.*"[6] (Martin was as liberal in the use of italics as he was of intoxicants. Herein I've saved the reader from enduring much, but not all, of Martin's eager emphasis.) He had been an organizer, along with future convention delegates Paterson and Oliver Ellsworth of Connecticut, who would abuse Martin in a postconvention open letter so stinging that its venom lingers to this day, of the puckishly named Well Meaning Society, whose meaning, perhaps, was understood all too well by the divines of the college, who suppressed the society and its rival, the Plain Dealing Society. (The Well Meaning Society resurfaced in 1770 as the Cliosophic Society, which to this day kisses up to influential personages.)

James Madison, Aaron Burr, Philip Freneau, Benjamin Rush: Princetonians were represented—how well we venture not to say—at the Founding. Nine delegates at Philadelphia were Princeton graduates. Republicans, if not Anti-Federalists, were grown at the College of New Jersey.

Immodestly, perhaps, Martin urged those who doubted his character to seek out his old classmates, for they would testify to "the friendliness of my disposition, the correctness of my manners . . . my assiduity in my studies . . . [and] my literary attainments."[7]

Martin was graduated from Princeton five months shy of his nineteenth birthday. His resolve "fixed upon the profession of law,"[8] he sought a position in Philadelphia, vainly. But in the course of application he learned that the master of the Free-School of Queen Anne's County on Maryland's Eastern Shore had recently dropped dead. He got the job. (A Reverend Keene, uncle of the rascal who would seduce Martin's daughter, was among the school's trustees.)

Viewing the teaching post as a temporary stop on the path to the bar, Martin plied the pedagogical arts at Queen Anne's until April 1770. We have no reason at this point to doubt his sobriety, but the improvidence that would beggar him till his dying day was already in evidence. Not that Martin felt any shame about his indebtedness. "I am not even yet," he wrote in 1802, "I was not *then*, nor have I *ever* been, an economist of anything but *time*." The cost of food, lodging, clothing, and a twenty-one-year-old's incidentals add up, so "No person will think it a matter of surprize [sic], much less of disgrace, that I did not rigidly restrain my expenditures to my income—or that a youth of my age, of a warm and generous heart, left so totally to his own guidance, should become indebted beyond his power of immediate payment."[9] Would that every spendthrift lad with a maxed-out credit card were as eloquent!

His creditors were unmoved. Five writs were served upon him. (Though his cumulative debts, he tells us, were a "paltry sum, not exceeding two hundred dollars!") In March 1770, they were "struck off" at the county court.[10] Martin left Queen Anne's County shortly thereafter. The venomous Keene would imply much later that Martin's path out of town was garlanded by drink and damsels, but this likely is a roorback, for Martin seems to have been well regarded by the superintending Board of Visitors. (In 1779, Martin would engage in a brief broadside war with a critic who suggested that the young teacher left town just ahead of an irate father. Martin sprayed his accuser with an impressive staccato of invective and added, primly, that he had overcome "the extreme reluctance, which I naturally have for news-paper controversies."[11] He professed to "hate controversies as I hate ratbane."[12] That didn't last long.)

Martin made his way down the Eastern Shore to Virginia, where he taught for a year at the unfortunately named Onancock Grammar School. By night he studied law, and in September 1771 he was examined at Williamsburg by the formidable duo of Virginia Attorney General John "the Tory" Randolph (not to be confused with the brilliant and eccentric Tertium Quid of the same name) and George Wythe, who in fewer than five years would sign the Declaration of Independence. Martin was granted license to practice in the county courts of Virginia. Thus began the career of "one of the ablest lawyers which our country has produced."[13]

The call of his ancestral Jersey home must have been dim indeed, for Martin determined upon a Virginia residence. In April 1772 the new lawyer traveled to Williamsburg as part of a tour "to determine on the place" where he might cast down his bucket.[14]

Here he befriended another garrulous Anti-Federalist of the future, Patrick Henry. For six months he ranged and reconnoitered through the Old Dominion, visiting friends and frontiersmen. Upon returning to the Eastern Shore he was informed that a trio of able lawyers had passed on to their rewards. New shingles were begging to be hanged. Luther Martin commenced his practice in four Eastern Shore counties, two in Virginia and two in Maryland. He made a home—for the nonce—in Somerset County, Maryland, natal place of the Maryland revolutionary Samuel Chase. Soon he was earning, by his own account, one thousand pounds per year, though as an economist of nothing but time, his creditors were never scarce.

His sympathies were squarely with the incipient revolution. In 1774 he was—"in my absence and without being consulted," he hastens to add—selected by the people of Somerset to serve as a delegate to a November statewide meeting in Annapolis that had been called by Maryland's Continental Congress delegation for the purpose of protesting British policies. Martin attended, and of his fervent patriotism he was ever proud. He was no sunshine patriot, waving flags as Johnny came marching home in victory; as he recalled in *Modern Gratitude*, "there was a period of considerable duration, throughout which, not only myself, but many others, acting in the same manner, did not lay down one night on their beds, without the hazard of waking on board a British armed ship, or in the other world."[15]

Martin fought the Revolution with writ, pen, handbill, and perhaps even blunderbuss. He distributed—"at great personal risk"—the first copies of Thomas Paine's *Common Sense* in Somerset County.[16] (He certainly would have agreed with Paine's famous distinction that "Society in every state is a blessing, but government, even in its best state, is but a necessary evil.")[17] He self-published and distributed his response (first appearing in the September 9, 1777, *Maryland Gazette*) to General William Howe's pledge that the king's army would not plunder the property or "molest the persons of any of his Majesty's WELL DISPOSED SUBJECTS."

No one ever accused Luther Martin of a well disposition; he fired back against the "cruel and deceitful enemy" and reprehended His Majesty's loyalists as "base coward[s]" who were the "enem[ies] to virtue and freedom."[18]

He would soon be in position to do something about it, if not on the field of battle (though he did serve, with something less than Valley Forge-ish arduousness, with the Baltimore Light Dragoons), then in the court of law. With the sponsorship of Samuel Chase, with whom Martin's career would intersect so many times over the years, he was appointed by Governor Thomas Johnson as attorney general of Maryland on February 11, 1778. He went after bellicose loyalists with especial vigor, but his conduct in office was generally praised.

As if coalescing the regions of his adopted state, the young Eastern Shore lawyer, now resident in Baltimore, wed the daughter of a prominent western Maryland frontier family. On Christmas Day, 1783, he married Maria Cresap, in whose home he had tarried during his postgraduate tour of the outback.

The details of Martin's attorney generalship, ably traced by Clarkson and Jett, are of limited interest to us. His courtroom comportment, however, is directly relevant. Contemporaneous observers conceded his considerable talents while dwelling on the unorthodox means he employed to achieve his goal. "Mr. Martin seemed indifferent to everything else, provided he impressed upon the Court the idea he wished to convey," recalled Roger B. Taney.

Martin lacked an internal editor; he spoke without organization, throwing out anything that might stick to its target. "Martin would plunge into a case when he had not even read the record," wrote Taney, "relying on the fulness of readiness of his own mind; and, if he found unexpected difficulties, would waste a day in a rambling, pointless, and wearisome speech against time, in order to gain a night to look into the case."[19]

We will hear more about wearisome two-day speeches.

By the mid-1780s, he was well on his way to becoming the state drunkard. Tales of his bibulosity are common, and as is often the case with tosspots they can partake of both pathos and humor, usually in some uneasy combination. In one trial he undertook a definition of his frequent condition: "A man is drunk when after drinking liquor he says or does that which he would not otherwise have said or done."[20] If true, it will not matter how much he drinks in the taverns of the City of Brotherly Love—he meant every word he said in Independence Hall.

Money, like alcohol, ran through Luther Martin. His "chief faults," according to the *Dictionary of American Biography*, "were his intemperance and his improvidence in financial affairs."[21] He never met a dollar worthy of saving. Martin's finances were as unsteady as a drunkard's gait. Having not the advantages of hereditary wealth or a nearby discount liquor store, making due as a schoolteacher and then a tyro lawyer, he was ever bobbing on a sea of indebtedness. This "want of economy in his pecuniary affairs," in James B. Longacre's cushiony phrase, "was prominent through life."[22]

Even a sympathetic historian called him "a profligate spendthrift of the worst type."[23] Yet he was not greedy, nor was he a chiseler. He cheated no man. He spent freely, though he sometimes

spent money he had not made. Not yet. But if the gentleman credi-
tor would just be patient, the prospects for repayment were favor-
able. Eftsoons, my good man, eftsoons. The check is in the mail.

If Martin took more interest in public affairs than he did in the
mere accumulation of material wealth, he did not submit to the
biblical injunction and take what he had and give to the poor. Like
other striving Maryland men, he bought properties confiscated
during the Revolution: four lots at 2,360 pounds from the estate of
an English merchant in April 1781; and with three other investors,
including Samuel Chase, he bought three lots that had been seized
from the Principio Company, absentee British landlords. Expro-
priating the expropriators, you might say. Of the 3,150 pounds he
had invested in confiscated property, almost 600 pounds remained
unpaid to the state treasury as of 1788.[24]

Martin, Chase, William Paca, and other Anti-Federalist speculators in confiscated land were often found on the paper money
side of financial debates in Maryland in the mid-1780s, a fact
seized upon by critics to establish that they, like virtually every
other public figure, may have voted on occasion in self-interest.
The debtors primarily owed British creditors and the tax collector—unsympathetic and, by some revolutionary reckonings, ille-
gitimate dunners. Petitioners from rural areas entreated the governor to "mitigate the rigors of tax collection."[25] Maryland courts
were clogged with debt suits; sheriffs and taxmen cut their confis-
catory swath through the distressed farmlands of the state.

As the economy slumped in the mid-1780s, the yeomanry—as
well as lawyers who had speculated none too shrewdly in real estate, such as Samuel Chase—demanded state issuance of cheap paper money by which these dubious debts might be retired. Even in
Maryland, by reputation oligarchic rather than populist, popular

resistance grew to writ and vendue. In best American fashion, the resistance blended the communal and the libertarian. Neighbors packed public auctions of property seized for nonpayment of taxes. Officers who aided in the confiscation of private property were threatened; tax collectors slept uneasily. The redemption songs of the Shaysites were borne on the night wind.

The Maryland House of Delegates and Senate were at protracted loggerheads over the issuance of paper money and the treatment of debtors. This wrangling was part of the reason why the leaders of the pro– and anti–paper money factions declined appointment to the Philadelphia convention of 1787. Which opened the door to Luther Martin.

The delegates did not gather in Philadelphia with a license to simply rip up the Articles of Confederation and start anew. The pertinent comma-tose congressional resolution of February 21, 1787, read: "Resolved that in the opinion of Congress it is expedient that on the second Monday in May next a Convention of delegates who shall have been appointed by the several states be held at Philadelphia *for the sole and express purpose of revising the Articles of Confederation* (my emphasis) and reporting to Congress and the several legislatures such alterations and provisions therein as shall when agreed to in Congress and confirmed by the states render the federal constitution adequate to the exigencies of Government & the preservation of the Union."[26]

In his elegant dissection *Our Enemy, the State* (1935), Albert Jay Nock terms the convention "a *coup d'Etat*, organized by methods which if employed in any other field than that of politics, would be put down at once as not only daring, but unscrupulous and dishonourable." With Beardian boldness, Nock charges the Founders with "simply tossing the Articles of Confederation into the wastebasket, and drafting a constitution de novo, with the audacious provision that it should go into effect when ratified by nine units instead of all thirteen."[27]

The Articles, drawn up and debated in Congress during the Revolutionary dawn of 1776–77, linked the thirteen states in "a firm league of friendship" to secure their liberties and the common defense.[28] The powers of this confederacy—the United States of America—were strictly limited, for the authors knew that "men in power naturally lusted for more power and that restraints must be put on officeholders or the liberties of the people would inevitably suffer."[29]

The states entered the confederation as perfect equals: each possessed a single vote in Congress, though their delegations might consist of between two and seven members. Significant legislation required a supermajority of nine votes; amendments required a unanimous thirteen. No person could serve in Congress for more than three years in any six-year period. Members could also be recalled at the pleasure of the states. The confederacy had not the power to regulate commerce or prohibit Rhode Island from issuing paper money or levy direct taxes on New Yorkers or any of a thousand other acts that the union would ultimately commit.

The Articles were rescued from ignominy and obscurity in the 1940s by University of Wisconsin colonial historian Merrill Jensen, a South Dakota farmboy whose populist sympathies and belief that "above all, the Revolution itself was a revolt against centralization of political authority" disposed him to view kindly the Articles of Confederation.[30]

"[T]he constitution which the radicals created, the Articles of Confederation, was a constitutional expression of the philosophy of the Declaration of Independence," wrote Merrill Jensen. It was libertarian in its suspicion of state power and decentralist in its preference for dispersed, localized governance. It was based in the "belief that democracy was possible only within fairly small political units whose electorate had a direct check upon the officers of government."[31]

In the social-studies textbook story of America, the Articles are written off as a failure. They were too mild by half, inadequately cohesive, comically unable to raise money from selfish states. As Merrill Jensen writes:

> The Articles of Confederation have been assigned one of the most inglorious roles in American history. They have been treated as the product of ignorance and inexperience and the parent of chaos; hence the necessity for a new constitution in 1787 to save the country from ruin. In so interpreting the first constitution of the United States and the history of the country during its existence, historians have accepted a tradition established by the Federalist Party. They have not stopped to consider that the Federalist Party was organized to destroy a constitution embodying ideals of self-government and economic practice that were naturally abhorrent to those elements in American society of which that party was the political expression.[32]

The competency of the Articles is beyond the scope of this book; suffice to say that Jensen had impressive company in the ranks of its defenders. The view in 1788 of South Carolina Anti-Federalist Rawlins Lowndes that the Articles were "a most excellent constitution . . . sent like a blessing from Heaven" and had "given to us the enviable blessings of liberty and independence" was shared by many of his coevals.[33]

Patrick Henry, among others, denied that the Articles needed an overhaul. Virginians, he said, were not "dissatisifed" with the confederation. They went about their daily business unaware of the alleged grievous faults of their lenient, gossamer-light government: "The middle and lower ranks of people have not those illuminated ideas which the well-born are so happily possessed of; they cannot so readily perceive latent objects. The microscopic eyes of modern statesmen"—calling Mr. Madison—"can see abundance of defects in old systems; and their illuminated imaginations discover the necessity of a change."[34]

James Madison, anticipating the Philadelphia convention, complained to Edmund Randolph on February 25, 1787, "Our situation is becoming every day more and more critical. No money comes into the federal treasury; no respect is paid to the federal authority." Leading men, he says, are speaking of monarchy; others envision a partition into "two or more confederacies."[35] It was time to crack the whip on the recalcitrant states.

The stakes, at least as conceived by centripetally inclined historians such as the influential John Fiske, were huge. Would the thirteen states combine under a unitary system to form a "single powerful and pacific nation" or would power be "parcelled out among forty or fifty small communities, wasting their strength and lowering their moral tone by perpetual warfare, like the states of ancient Greece, or by perpetual preparation for warfare, like the nations of modern Europe."[36] Not that Fiske was taking sides, you see.

The equality of state suffrage under the Articles was an obstacle to those who dreamt of assertive nationalism. Undisturbed, it may well have led to a union of smaller, fissioned states, for as Peter S. Onuf points out, "because of equal state voting under the Articles, the large states would not sacrifice any political advantage by becoming smaller; on the contrary, assuming some harmony of interest within its original boundaries, the division of a large state into two or more states would increase its effective voting strength."[37] Upper New York, New York City, West Massachusetts, Upcountry Carolina—oh, the states we might have had.

Martin's Maryland was the last state to ratify the Articles, largely because as a "landless state"—unlike her neighbor Virginia, which had collops and wattles and dewlaps of claimed land—she wished to grant Congress power over the states' western boundaries. The Articles, in providing that "no State shall be deprived of territory for the benefit of the United States," seemed to acknowledge the claims of Virginia and other land-greedy states to vast tracts west of the Appalachians, even to the Pacific Ocean. These ultramontane territories, insisted the representatives of Maryland, Delaware, and New Jersey, ought to be the common property of the states that fought and won the Revolution.

Maryland did not assent to the Articles until March 1781, after Congress had resolved that new states, equal in rights to the original thirteen, were to be carved out of the lands of the west. Of her obstinate refusal to ratify, New Hampshire Continental Congress delegate William Whipple wrote that "there now only remains Maryland who you know has seldom done anything with a good Grace. She has always been a froward hussey."[38] The hussey suspected the intentions of the cavalier next door: Virginia, she thought, would replenish, again and again, its treasury through sales of her limitless acreage, "lessen her taxes" with the proceeds, and attract settlers from higher-tax neighbors such as Maryland.[39]

Sometimes froward, not forward, is the wisest course.

Six years later, the conspicuous honor of being chosen a delegate to the Philadelphia convention seems to have escaped the notice of many prominent Maryland men. Samuel Chase and William Paca removed themselves from consideration early. Charles Carroll of Carrollton, a Roman Catholic, a Federalist, and the wealthiest man and biggest slaveowner in Maryland, refused the honor. A quintet was finally selected in April, but only one of the chosen, Baltimore physician and Federalist James McHenry, accepted. On May 22, the legislature filled out the delegation with four replacements: John Francis Mercer, only twenty-eight, who had studied law with Jefferson and who would usually vote but not vocalize with Martin; the prepositionally named Daniel of St. Thomas Jenifer, erstwhile agent for the Lords Baltimore, proprietors of the colony of Maryland; Daniel Carroll, cousin of Charles and political kindred, too: and Luther Martin. It was a delegation of middling reputation.

There is some irony in the fact that Maryland, by reputation one of the most aristocratic and least democratic states, a place name redolent not of Minutemen but of coxcomb barons, dispatched the single most radical delegate to Philadelphia.

Property qualifications restricted the franchise as well as eligibility to hold public office; Maryland state senators were chosen by an electoral college, an arrangement praised by Madison in *Federalist 63*. These antidemocratic features combined "to safeguard property rights and the interests of the upper economic and social class from any attack whatsoever," wrote historian Philip A. Crowl.[40]

Here as elsewhere, the country party, centered in the lower house, the House of Delegates, had been the party of revolution, of self-government, against the peruke-topped fops and lords man-qué of the Senate. Maryland boasted, by general agreement, the finest bar in the colonies and a "litigious spirit."[41] Her litigators lit the lamp of independence and liberty.

First among equals in the country party was Samuel Chase, Annapolis lawyer, Declaration signatory, and paper-money advo-cate. Few men were pococurante about Samuel Chase. Son of a Catholic-baiting Church of England priest, avaricious speculator ever alert to the main chance or even a minor one, coarse social climber sensitive to slights from the gentry, Chase was disprized in gentlemanly circles. If he was not quite a crook, he did have a knack for promoting legislation from which he would benefit handsomely. Yet as one contemporary wrote: "vile as Chase has been held by most of the better kind of his fellow Citizens, he has been the mover of almost every thing, this State has to boast of. Strange inconsistent man!"[42]

He was a patriot firebrand, an early, vocal, and brave advocate of American independence. Much less radical than his reputation, he sought strict property qualifications for suffrage, longer terms, and more appointive offices. He wanted to be a grandee. But like Luther Martin, he lived habitually beyond his means, investing heavily in confiscated Tory property. Charles Carroll of Carroll-ton called him "the most prostitute scoundrel, who ever existed."[43] In 1778, he was accused—plausibly, but without the presence of a smoking gun—of passing inside information from Congress to his partners so that they might buy hugely in wheat and flour in anticipation of a large purchase thereof by the commissary gen-eral. Alexander Hamilton, writing as "Publius" of Poughkeepsie in 1778, damned Chase as "a traitor of the worst and most dan-gerous kind," a man to be "immortalised in infamy. . . . The love of money and the love of power are the predominating ingredients of [his] mind."[44] And yet, as we shall see, Chase—patriot and plunger—was to be a cause célèbre of the Hamiltonian Federalists a quarter-century later.

Chase's absence from the Maryland delegation put the ball in Luther Martin's hands. He was not afraid to shoot.

Chase and the other men who ought to have been the leaders of what we might call the libertarian decentralist party were not in Philadelphia: Patrick Henry had refused to come, saying that he "smelt a rat."[45] Richard Henry Lee begged off for reasons of health. Sam Adams was back in Massachusetts. Willie Jones of North Carolina said he was too busy. Thomas Jefferson was in France. New York's George Clinton sent Robert Yates and John Lansing in his stead. Rhode Island, proud and obstinate and Anti-Federal as all hell, if not all providence, never did send delegates: as its general assembly informed Congress, little Rhodey was acting upon "that great principle which hath ever been the characteristic of this state, the love of true constitutional liberty, and the fear we have of making innovations on the rights and liberties of the citizens at large."[46] And so it fell to Luther Martin, the brash young parvenu, the prolix toper, the man who would not shut up, to make the case against the Constitution. And he did so with a power and cogency that no one would ever bother to equal. He lacked the prestige and pull of the aforementioned men, but he had guts in abundance.

The average age of the fifty-five delegates to the Philadelphia convention was forty-two, which put Martin in the younger set. About three-quarters had served in Congress (Martin had been elected by the Maryland legislature to serve in Congress in 1785, though he never sat with the body); thirty-four were lawyers. Important hotbeds of localist and libertarian passion—the western sections of Massachusetts and Pennsylvania, all of Rhode Island—were, fatefully, unrepresented.

Attendance was desultory. Perhaps thirty members were present on a typical day. Sessions ran every day but Sunday from ten forenoon till three or four in the afternoon. On Monday, May 14, the day fixed for the convention's opening, "a small number only had assembled,"[47] according to Madison, so the kickoff was pushed back till Friday, May 25, on which day majorities of seven delegations were present at Independence Hall. George Washington of Virginia was unanimously elected chairman. He would say little within the convention proper, but his conviction, as expressed in an August 1786 letter to John Jay, would carry the day: "I do not conceive we can exist long as a nation without having lodged somewhere a power, which will pervade the whole Union in as energetic a manner, as the authority of the State Governments extends over the several States."[48]

(Although Martin's contempt for the more abstract theorizers of the Federalist faction he barely bothered to hide, he always revered Washington. Even in the heat of the ratification battles he declared, "The name of Washington is far above my praise.")[49]

Rules were adopted on the following Monday and Tuesday, among them this injunction to silence: "That nothing spoken in the House be printed, or otherwise published or communicated without leave."[50] The deliberations were to be secret, shielded from the prying eyes of the citizenry. Armed sentries barred admission to the rabblement. What happens in Philadelphia stays in Philadelphia. Statesmanship, or so the conceit had it, is best practiced in a cloister.

Luther Martin, who would not arrive for another fortnight, denied that seclusion was good policy. 'Twas a foul spirit indeed that "caused our doors to be shut, our proceedings to be kept secret,—our journals to be locked up,—and every avenue, as far as possible, to be shut to public information."[51] Jefferson, writing from Paris, also bemoaned "so abominable a precedent as that of tying up the tongues of their members."[52] (Jefferson and Martin would come to loathe each other. Jefferson accused Martin's father-in-law, Captain Michael Cresap, of murdering the family of an Indian chief named Logan. Martin, dutiful son-in-law, took to his meal ticket's defense, and the feud was on. Of such slights and piques is history made. Jefferson tagged Martin with an enduring nickname when he called him an "unprincipled and imprudent federal bull-dog."[53] For his part, Martin had no greater insult in his quiver than to say that a man was "as great a scoundrel as Tom Jefferson.")[54]

It took a couple of weeks for the lay of the land to reveal itself. Martin was later to tell the Maryland legislature that the convention was divided into three factions: "one were for abolishing all the State Governments; another for such a Government as would give an influence to particular States—and a third party were truly Federal,"[55] seeking ways to shore up the modest weaknesses of the Articles whilst protecting liberty and guarding against the malign designs of the other two. The first, and smallest, faction, had as its dissembling paragon Alexander Hamilton of New York. The second, which in eventual league with the archcentralists would dominate the convention, was Virginia-based, with James Madison at its head. The third, the beleaguered patriots of '76, gathered around Martin and the plan advanced by his Princeton classmate, William Paterson of New Jersey.

The delegates misreflected public attitudes, at least judging by the closeness of many of the state conventions that later ratified the Constitution. William H. Riker and Evelyn Fink have estimated that nationally the electorate was split 50–46 in favor of the Constitution, which "called for a more centralized government than the median voter would have preferred." But the conclave that produced the charter was lopsidedly nationalist. Those favoring quasi-monarchic measures (a lifetime term for the president) or the outright abolition of the states were as numerous, if not more so, than those representing the localist, decentralist, libertarian tradition that would be identified with (the pre- and postpresidential) Thomas Jefferson. As Riker marveled, "The ideological homogeneity of the convention is astonishing."[56]

The consolidationists took the initiative. On May 29, dithering frontman Edmund Randolph introduced the Virginia Plan—the template upon which the counterrevolution of 1787 was based. "The plan was undoubtedly written by Madison," wrote Irving Brant, the primary biographer of the diminutive Sage of Montpelier.[57] Brant is a fierce and able partisan for his man, and in this assertion he is no doubt correct.

Edmund Randolph was the suave Virginia governor of whom Max Farrand wrote, "As a leader he was wanting in decision, as a figurehead he was splendid."[58] Curiously, Randolph would later refuse to sign the document, explaining—in a letter that even its author conceded to be "tedious"—that he wished the state conventions to suggest amendments which might be taken up by a second General Convention. He objected, particularly, to the equality of suffrage in the Senate and the extensive grant of powers to the president.[59] Yet he turned coat once more and helped shepherd the Constitution's passage through the Virginia ratification convention of June 1788.

The Randolph-Madison Virginia Plan provided for a bicameral national legislature, with representation in each house reflecting a state's population or its contributions to the national treasury. The first house was elected by the people of the states; the second was chosen by the first, from a list of candidates submitted by the state legislatures. A single-headed executive and a national judiciary consisting of superior and inferior tribunals were also to be created; an admixture of these two branches formed a "Council of revision" to review acts of the legislature. The plan was a lineation, full of blanks and lacunae to be filled in later, but it was a working document for the counterrevolution.

The principle of equal suffrage, cornerstone of the Articles, had been discarded. In the Randolph-Madison Senate, three states (Virginia, Pennsylvania, Massachusetts) would supply thirteen of the twenty-eight members.

Most audaciously, the Virginia Plan enabled the national government "to negative all laws passed by the several States, contravening in the opinion of the National Legislature the articles of Union."[60] This was the prized brainchild of James Madison, who even before the convention had demanded, "Let [the national government] have a negative, in all cases whatsoever, on the legislative acts of the states, as the king of Great Britain heretofore had. This I conceive to be essential. . . . Let this national supremacy be extended also to the judiciary department."[61] With this one clause, so implacably contrary to the spirit of the Articles of Confederation (if slightly narrower than Madison's absolutist desideratum), the Virginians were proposing to neuter the state governments, or as New York Anti-Federalist delegate Robert Yates phrased it in his notes, Randolph "meant a strong, consolidated union, in which the idea of States should be nearly annihilated."[62]

Yates did not misrepresent the national negative. If Madison sought not the legal abolition of the states, he was nonetheless ardent for their effectual nullification. Plotting—or rather dictating—strategy with Edmund Randolph on April 8, he had insisted, as a "fundamental point," upon the "due supremacy of the national authority," though he would "leave in force the local authorities so far as they can be subordinately useful."

So far as they can be subordinately useful. This was counterrevolution, as Madison understood. "In truth," he said—privately, natch, and not in public, not even in that severely circumscribed public that was the Philadelphia convention, wrapped in secrecy as a corpse is sheathed in cerecloth—"my ideas of a reform strike so deeply at the old Confederation, and lead to such a systematic change," as to amount to an overthrow.[63] (My word—Madison wasn't *that* truthful.)

"There is a tendency," wrote Charles F. Hobson, editor of the Madison Papers at the University of Virginia, "to assume an identity between Madison the Convention deputy and Madison the author of the 'Publius' essays" of *The Federalist Papers*,[64] yet the federalism of the latter—milksop as it was—is hardly anticipated by the consolidationist at Philadelphia.

The consolidators rolled merrily along in their "nationalist assault," encountering resistance chiefly along the large state/small state divide. But on June 9, discord—"driving fanaticism" (Irving Brant)—blew into the hall.[65] Luther Martin—"unquestionably the most curious figure at the Constitutional Convention," as Christopher and James Lincoln Colllier wrote in *Decision in Philadelphia*—was in the house.[66]

Martin was, uncharacteristically, "silent in disbelief at what he had heard."[67] The Convention, working from the Virginia Plan, was scrapping the Articles of Confederation and supplanting it with a consolidated national government.

Nine months later, Martin described his first days among the immortals:

> It was on Saturday that I first took my seat. I obtained that day a copy of the propositions that had been laid before the Convention, and which were then the subject of discussion in a committee of the whole. The Secretary was so polite as, at my request, to wait upon me at the State House the next day (being Sunday), and there gave me an opportunity of examining the journals and making myself acquainted with the little that had been done before my arrival. I was not a little surprised at the system brought forward, and was solicitous to learn the reasons which had been assigned in its support; for this purpose the journals could be of no service; I therefore conversed on the subject with different members of the Convention, and was favoured with minutes of the debates which had taken place before my arrival.

The grog shops could wait.

> I applied to history for what lights it could afford me, and I procured everything the most valuable I could find in Philadelphia on the subject of governments in general, and on the American revolution and governments in particular. I devoted my whole time and attention to the business in which we were engaged, and made use of all the opportunities I had, and abilities I possessed, conscientiously to decide what part I ought to adopt in the discharge of that sacred duty I owed to my country. . . . I attended the Convention many days without taking any share in the debates, listening in silence to the eloquence of others, and offering no other proof that I possessed the powers of speech, than giving my yea or nay when a question was taken.[68]

Well, he wasn't exactly mute in those first days. On Monday the 11th, Martin made his first motion: to strike the requirement that state officials take an oath "to support the articles of Union."[69] He lost, seven states to four. It was the first loss of many.

In accounts of the convention, Martin is sometimes given a walk-on role as an obstructionist, a naysayer. Just what is so ignoble about saying no to what one thinks is a ruinous course is unclear, but in any event Martin was brimful of ideas—it's just that they didn't lead to a leviathan on the Potomac. Catherine Drinker Bowen sniffed that Martin's was one of those "minds offended by novelty."[70] This is the time-honored jibe at those who balk at any triumphant innovation: You can't stop Progress! Don't even try, mossback!

But Martin did more than just say no.

He hadn't been in town for a sennight before contributing to, if not serving as an uncredited subauthor of, the primary alternative to the Virginia Plan: the New Jersey Plan, the truly federal alternative, the path not taken, the decentralist alternative to the ultimately victorious Constitution.

It seems likely—though we lack proof—that Luther Martin, his college chum William Paterson, Roger Sherman of Connecticut ("awkward, un-meaning, and unaccountably strange in his manner," whistled Georgia's William Pierce),[71] and perhaps John Lansing of New York and John Dickinson of Delaware traded ideas as part of an ad hoc small state/states' rights caucus. (Dickinson was no localist, but the Delaware legislature had explicitly instructed her delegates to resist any alteration in the equality of state suffrage.)

If New York seems an odd element of the small-state alliance, recall not only that two-thirds of her delegation (Lansing and

Yates) were staunch Anti-Federalists but also that New York was not so much a large state as it was the largest of the midsized states. In the anticipated House apportionment, New York had six of the sixty-five representatives, fewer than Virginia (ten) and Pennsylvania and Massachusetts (eight apiece) and the same as Maryland. Connecticut, usually credited (or blamed) as leader of the small states, would have five representatives, the same as both Carolinas.

A word about the fractious New Yorkers. John Lansing Jr. and Robert Yates represented liberty-minded Upstate New York, while their colleague Alexander Hamilton spoke for the mercantilists and monarchists of the City.

Judge Yates, Schenectady-born and -bred, was "the *honest lawyer*," as an anonymous biographer in 1821 called him, noting that he died broke.[72] (So would Martin.) Lansing, thirty-three years of age when the convention met, had studied law with Yates and had already served in Congress and as Speaker of the New York Assembly. He would, in time, succeed Yates as chief justice of the New York Supreme Court and later serve as chancellor of the state of New York. His was a distinguished career with a bizarre and mysterious end. In 1829, the elderly Anti-Federalist Lansing disappeared into a New York City evening, never to be seen again. He may have fallen from a pier (he had left his hotel to post a letter on a boat bound for Albany); perhaps cutpurses robbed and killed him. Thurlow Weed, the cunning political operative who was then manipulating the Anti-Masonic movement in Upstate New York, claimed darkly that Lansing was killed for knowing too much.

James Madison would not have desired Lansing's death, but he wouldn't have minded if the majority of the New York delegation had disappeared into the Philadelphia night. "Colonel Hamilton, with a Mr. Yates and a Mr. Lansing, are appointed by New York,"

Madison wrote Edmund Randolph on March 11, 1787. "The two latter are supposed to lean too much towards state considerations to be good members of an assembly which will only be useful in proportion to its superiority to partial views and interests."[73] Little Jemmy, the universal man, the farsighted abstractionist, was already impatient with the earthbound clodhoppers from Upstate New York.

Yates and Lansing left Philadelphia in disgust on July 10. They explained their early departure in a letter to Governor George Clinton.

Philadelphia, it seems, offered only a rock and a hard place. Realizing that they had been "reduced to the disagreeable alternative of either exceeding the powers delegated to us, and giving assent to measures which we conceive destructive to the political happiness of the citizens of the United States, or opposing our opinions to that of a body of respectable men," they caught the first coach back to New York.

The conventioneers were not merely "revising the Articles of Confederation," as they had been charged to do; no, they were "establishing a general government, pervading every part of the United States," which Lansing and Yates considered an "impracticability" that would lead to "the destruction of the civil liberty of such citizens who could be effectually coerced by it."[74]

The scale was all wrong. Thirteen far-flung states could not be ruled from one federal city. Lansing called the Constitution "a triple-headed monster, as deep and wicked a conspiracy as ever was invented in the darkest ages against the liberties of a free people."[75]

(If William Pierce can be credited, the loss to Anti-Federalist forensics was bearable. Yates, asserted the Georgia Federalist, was "not distinguished as an Orator," and Lansing "has a hisitation

[sic] in his speech, that will prevent his being an Orator of any eminence;—his legal knowledge, I am told is not extensive, nor his education a good one.")[76]

The third New Yorker, and perhaps the delegate who least reflected the views of his state, was Alexander Hamilton. How apt that Hamilton is enjoying a vogue in our own day just as his archrival Jefferson is experiencing a slough! For the West Indian bastard envisioned a centralized, militarized empire stoked by the perpetual fires of finance capitalism. (Do I descend into name-calling? Ah, I merely follow the trodden path. For Hamilton and associates had derided as an "old Booby" Yates's uncle Abraham, the Albany shoemaker and Anti-Federalist, the lawyer-cobbler who sometimes wrote under the pseudonym "Rough Hewer" and damned the men who "turned a *Convention* into a *Conspiracy*, and under the Epithet *Federal* have destroyed the Confederation.")[77]

Since New York had stipulated that two of its three delegates constituted a quorum, the absence of Lansing and Yates deprived the Anti-Federalists of a reliable vote. It also gave James Madison the last historical word on the proceedings of the convention. For there in the front of the room sat scribbling away the Man in Black. According to Pierce, Madison dressed all in black at Philadelphia in what was, I am reasonably sure, not an homage to Johnny Cash. Yes, he walked the line, but it was a nationalizing line, and those who chose other paths were tossed into the burning ring of fire. In his notes on the convention, Madison wrote cattily that Luther Martin spoke "with much diffuseness and considerable vehemence."[78] It is in part from Madison's account that Martin has earned his reputation as the most voluble delegate.

Yet the hypochondriacal Madison, a valetudinarian who could out-kvetch the worst whiner in the nursing home, is hardly an irreproachable amanuensis. "He took his work so seriously that it seemed to have stifled any sense of humor he is said to have possessed and deprived his notes of any enlivening qualities," wrote Max Farrand, hardly a revisionist firebrand.[79] Madison was also a partisan, a thoroughgoing nationalist at the time, despite his later move Jeffersonward. His transcriptions do not always do justice to the other side.

Madison's notes were published in 1840, four years after his death. They are the standard account of the convention, and with good reason: they are a stenographic marvel. But Judge Yates, too, kept notes, though since he and Lansing departed Philadelphia in early July they are of course incomplete, ending with a sputter on July 5. (Lansing kept notes until July 9. Both men attended the convention on July 10 for a last time.) During Yates's life "he conceived himself under honorable obligations to withhold their publication,"[80] but upon his death his widow permitted them to be published in 1821 as a corrective, of sorts, to *The Federalist Papers* and the official but frustratingly spare *Journal, Acts and Proceedings of the Convention, . . . which formed the Constitution of the United States*, which Secretary of State John Quincy Adams had prepared for publication in 1819. Madison disparaged Yates's published notes as a "very erroneous edition of the matter,"[81] though Farrand points out that in revising his own notes more than thirty years after the convention, Madison borrowed upwards of fifty quotations from Yates. We shall have more to say of these variorum accounts.

But back to the fork in the American road. William Paterson asked on June 14 for an adjournment, promising that on the morrow he would present a "purely federal" plan as an alternative to the Randolph-Madison scheme.[82]

On June 15, Paterson introduced the New Jersey Plan: the tantalizing path not taken. It modified the Articles, which after all was the ostensible purpose of the convention, and provided Congress with the means to raise revenue through tariffs and postage. Congress would remain unicameral, with an equal vote for each state, but a new wrinkle was a plural executive, chosen by Congress for a single fixed term and removable by Congress if so directed by a majority of state governors. "[I]t would seem," wrote Farrand, "as if the New Jersey Plan more nearly represented what most of the delegates supposed that they were sent to do."[83]

Sponsor William Paterson, born in Ireland, was a shopkeeper's son raised in Princeton and thus a townie, if you'll excuse the anachronism, at the College of New Jersey. He disapproved of the frivolous fops around him and set about, somewhat pompously, on becoming a gentleman. (Treat "inferiors . . . with Generosity and humanity, but by no means with Familiarity," wrote the merchant's boy in his college notebook.)[84] Competent and ambitious, he rose in the world, becoming attorney general of New Jersey. A "small-state nationalist," his biographer calls him,[85] though in Paterson's first significant address to the convention (June 9) he served notice upon the Randolph-Madison faction that their overreach would not go unchallenged. Madison gives a dull rendition of Paterson's speech; in Yates we find more eloquence: "We are met here as the deputies of thirteen independent, sovereign States, for federal purposes. Can we consolidate their sovereignty and form one nation, and annihilate the sovereignties of our States, who have sent us here for other purposes?"[86]

The forces of liberty and decentralism, the Spirit of '76, rallied to the New Jersey Plan. On June 16, Lansing of New York contrasted the Virginia and New Jersey blueprints: the former "involves a total Subversion of State Sovereignties," while the latter is in accord with federal principles.[87] Paterson, perhaps tired of the windy abstractions of Pennsylvanian James Wilson and Madison, remarked that "a little practical virtue is to be preferred to the finest theoretical principles."[88] Experience taught that confederations were most harmonious and respectful of liberty when member states had an equal vote. Why sacrifice the time-tested upon the altar of theory?

James Wilson, the deracinated Scot, responded with an ode to political giantism. "Why," he asked, "should a National Government be unpopular?" After all, "Will a Citizen of *Delaware* be degraded by becoming a Citizen of the *United States?*" On the contrary, the lesson of Great Britain is "that the smallest bodies . . . are notoriously the most corrupt."[89]

It was at this stage that Alexander Hamilton delivered the longest single-day speech of the convention, a six-hour chin-depresser on June 18. Madison, who would prove so ready to denigrate Martin as long-winded, records Hamilton's address smirklessly.

Hamilton announced himself "unfriendly" to both the Virginia and New Jersey plans. The latter was especially noxious, as it left "the States in possession of their Sovereignty."[90]

"[F]ederal governments," lectured Hamilton, "are weak and distracted." They are incapable of what in our age the imperialists call "national greatness." So "we must establish a general and national government, completely sovereign, and annihilate the State distinctions and State operations."[91] (This is from Yates; Madison chose to condense, paraphrase, or just plain squelch this passage.)

Hamilton is remarkably frank (but where is Reynolds?) about his desideratum: to "extinguish State Governments." He concedes its political impractibility: "It will not do to propose formal Extinction of State Governments—It would shock Public Opinion too much."[92] But as Madison records, "he saw no *other* necessity for declining it."

Even more shocking to the hoi polloi, had the convention not been veiled in secrecy, was Hamilton's monarchism. "In his private opinion," wrote Madison, "he had no scruple in declaring . . . that the British Gov. was the best in the world: and that he doubted much whether any thing short of it would do in America."[93] The monarch, he imagines, "can have no distinct interests from the public welfare."[94] The House of Lords is far superior to any "temporary Senate."[95]

Hamilton submitted an outline of his proposal to the convention, though it seems never to have been seriously discussed. He called for a bicameral legislature to consist of a popularly elected Assembly and a Senate whose members, chosen by electors, would serve for life. His executive, or governor, chosen by electors, also held a lifetime appointment; only a man so equipped "dares execute his powers."[96] This elective monarch—Hamilton accepted the term—would have an absolute veto over all legislation. As with the Virginia Plan, the central government could nullify state laws. State governors were to be appointed by the national government. Power was concentrated in the center and wielded by men who, once elected, were in for life. Hamilton stood at antipodes from Luther Martin and the decentralist Anti-Federalists. You will notice which man is on the ten-spot.

Gouverneur Morris adjudged Hamilton's exposition "the most able and impressive he had ever heard."[97] No doubt he spoke fluently, though if the blackout were not in effect the speech would have ruined Hamilton's career. As it was, he would dissemble about his convention role for the rest of his life.

Taking up the cudgel for theoretical principles, on the fateful day of June 19 Madison launched into an extraordinarily long disquisition—lengthier, perhaps, than any Martin speech, though Madison's notes make no reference to his own verbosity—on the defects of the New Jersey Plan. It failed, he complained, to bar states from issuing paper money or "encroach[ing] on the federal authority" and left "the will of the States as uncontrouled [sic] as ever." Madison warned balefully that if the convention broke up—as it would if the "inadmissible" (who died and made him arbiter of admissibility?) New Jersey Plan were adopted—the Union would dissolve, and the smaller states would be easy prey for the predations of the larger.[98] You may take that as a threat if you wish.

Whereupon the key vote of the convention was taken. I refer not to the famous Connecticut Compromise, approved on July 16, which provided for equality of representation in the Senate, but rather the vote of June 19 on Rufus King's motion that the New Jersey Plan was "not admissible"[99] and that, in Madison's phrase, "Mr. Randolph's [plan] should be adhered to as preferable to those of Mr. Paterson."[100]

By a vote of seven states (Massachusetts, Connecticut, Pennsylvania, Virginia, North Carolina, South Carolina, Georgia) to three (New York, New Jersey, Delaware), with Maryland divided, the convention approved King's motion. The nationalizing Virginia Plan was to be the markup document. (Note well, my Yankee and southern friends, that the Middle Atlantic states fought the good Anti-Federalist fight.)

A poet who wrote and lived just north of Boston, a Grover Cleveland Democrat, an Anti-Federalist of sorts, wrote about roads not taken. Imagining those roads can be as frustrating as it is stimulating. What if, one wonders. What if?

My beloved old University of Rochester professor William H. Riker, father of the school of positive political theory (he ought to have gotten the Nobel, but it's more important to be noble), once committed an exercise in speculative "social-science fiction" for Nelson Polsby's *What If?* (1982). Riker's question: "What if Elbridge Gerry Had Been More Rational and Less Patriotic?" Which is to say, what if Gerry, and by extension Massachusetts, had not voted for the Report of the Committee of Eleven (the Connecticut, or Great, Compromise) on July 16? (Of which more anon.) By voting aye, Gerry and his colleague Caleb Strong produced an equal division within the Bay State delegation, thus discounting the vote of Massachusetts and causing the report to be approved by a vote of 5–4. The convention was saved.

What if Gerry had voted no, as he had on previous considerations of the question? The convention would have broken up, in all likelihood, and since no pressing external threat would have prompted a quick reconvening, the states would have continued under the mild oversight of the Articles of Confederation. What if, asks Riker, there had been no Constitution?

Professor Riker limns a North America that looks rather like South America: a continent of countries, variously industrial, agrarian, slaveowning, Catholic. Bill Riker was a great admirer of Madison; he imagines the Constitution-less alternative world to consist of warring North American regional federations: a Confederacy of New England, a sprawling Louisiana, an independent Texas and California, a haughty Virginia, a Confederacy of the South in which slavery survived "well into the twentieth century," and others. Each would have been, in some measure, a republic, but the "most significant difference from what actually occurred . . . would be in the role of America in the world." The influence of these disconnected republics on world affairs would hardly be greater than that of the nations of South America.

"I know for certain," writes Riker, "that the relatively smaller and weaker American nations would not have been able to participate in European wars." An America-less First World War—or Great War, as we'd be calling it—would have ended in a German triumph, according to Riker. "There would, of course, have been no occasion for Hitler and the Second World War," and in carving up European Russia the Germans would have unwittingly prevented the rise of Soviet communism.[101]

No Constitution means no Hitler, no Stalin . . . and no American Civil War, for that matter. *This is dystopia*?

With a nod to Professor Riker, I offer my own what if. What if delegates from the Anti-Federalist states of New Hampshire and Rhode Island had been present on June 19? What if the Anti-Federalist Mercer had been there to tip Maryland's vote? What if Connecticut had flipped? With a tweak here and Gerry-like epiphany there, with a more representative New Hampshire delegation than the Granite State nationalists who actually showed up and maybe a timely attack of gout thrown in for good measure, what if enough votes had shifted so that the New Jersey Plan, and not the Virgina Plan, had been the markup document at the convention? What if the wise men of Philadelphia had not scrapped the Articles but had cleaved to its decentralist path, suitably redrawn? Would a monument (modest, naturally) to Paterson greet the occasional visitor to the sleepy federal city of . . . wait; there would be no federal city. Congress would meet, probably in Philadelphia, where the plural executives—the co-presidents of the United States, whose names the citizens never can quite recall—also keep their spartan offices. Luther Martin might stagger through histories of the early

Republic not as a contumacious dipsomaniac but as a charmingly dissipated defender of the confederation, rather as Franklin comes to us as a lovable roué.

Snap out of it, Bill!

"[T]he Nationalist party," wrote historian Charles Warren, had "secured a great triumph in the vote to adhere to the Virginia Plan for the new Government."[102] The die had been cast. The outline of history had been penciled in.

The archnationalists Wilson, Hamilton, and King were the first to speak after this epochal vote. Then Luther Martin rose. He was conceding no defeat. He had not yet begun to fight.

"When the States threw off their allegiance to Great Britain, they became independent of her and each other," Martin declared. (I quote from Yates, who as usual renders Martin with greater concinnity than Madison.) "They united and confederated for mutual defence; and this was done on principles of perfect reciprocity. They will not again meet on the same ground. But when a dissolution takes place, our original rights and sovereignties are resumed. Our accession to the Union has been by States. If any other principle is adopted by this convention," said Martin, I "will give it every opposition."[103]

Wilson and Hamilton immediately denied Martin's premise. The convention adjourned until the morrow. The game was on.

The Texas historian Mel Bradford discerned two strains of Anti-Federalism: "old-fashioned Whigs who thought that the Revolution had been fought to preserve the autonomy of local communities from the designs of a remote and arbitrary power; and those who wanted fiat money, a moratorium on the payment of debt, and direct democracy. Both types of Antifederalists demanded that a bill of rights be included or added to the Constitution. . . ."[104]

Luther Martin—the first Anti-Federalist, or at least a member of the first trio of Anti-Federalists with Lansing and Yates—was a sort of pan-Anti. Like Whitman, he contained multitudes. He spoke the language of localism, the language of liberty. He was a republican, not a democrat, but he spoke for the debtor class of small farmers who favored paper money and the abolition of imprisonment for debt. He spoke the language of small-f federalism, except that his side was bested in the name game. As the sympathetic historian Jackson Turner Main wrote, "They are called Antifederalists, but it should be made clear at once that they were not antifederal at all. . . . The attachment to them of a word which denotes the reverse of their true beliefs, and which moreover implies that they were mere obstructionists, without any positive plan to offer, was part of the penalty of defeat. The victors took what name they chose, and fastened on the losers one which condemned them."[105]

The name-switch was not uncontested. The Antis had been beaten to the punchy moniker, and they knew it. Melancton Smith, the gifted New Yorker who tilted with Hamilton throughout the New York convention, said that he hoped the Constitution-backers "would be complaisant enough to exchange names with those who disliked the Constitution, as it appeared . . . that they were federalists, and those who advocated it were anti-federalists."[106] No such luck.

Martin and his Anti-Federalist comrades viewed the United States as a confederation of sovereign states. Thus, Martin proposed a unicameral national legislature—one house—in which each state would have one vote. Members thereof would be selected by the state legislatures. Bicameralism made sense at the state level, said Martin, for state governments are entrusted with the protection of individual liberties. A skillful counterpoise of democratic and aristocratic influences in a lower and upper house may be the best guard against "oppression and injury."[107] But a federal government is formed by sovereign states and acts only upon those states, not upon individuals. It is no arena for the clash of classes. One house is sufficient. A second house is a redundancy. Nay, it is a Trojan Horse, for though it appears to be a further check upon tyranny in fact it provides cover for the encroachment of the federal government into the territory of the states.

On its surface, the Senate created by the Constitution, its members chosen by state legislatures, has a federal appearance, but on closer inspection this is the most ephemeral rouge. For senators serve six-year terms, the annual elections under the Articles having been scrapped. They are paid by the federal treasury rather than by the states which they putatively represent. And they are not subject to recall. Thus "for six years the senators are rendered totally and absolutely independent of their States."[108] Their paymaster in the federal city, predicted Martin, will absorb their energies and loyalties.

The Philadelphia delegates, Martin protested, "appeared totally to have forgot the business for which we were sent." They "had not been sent to form a government over the inhabitants of America, considered as individuals." Rather, they were "entrusted to prepare . . . a government over these thirteen States."[109] Somehow the states had been bypassed. Centralism was run amok.

The sole purpose, really, of the union was common defense and the protection of "the lesser states against the ambition of the larger."[110] Keeping Virginia in line. Virtually all other matters ought to be resolved at the state or local level.

Republican government, said Martin, "is only suited to a small and compact territory."[111] Luther Martin was a Marylander before he was an American. This ordering of loyalties is a useful way to separate Anti-Federalists from Federalists. Or, today, to distinguish localists from nationalists. For a lot of reasons, most prominently the hypermobility that is the curse of our lorn and lovely land, most of our countrymen in the early twenty-first century consider themselves Americans before they are New Englanders or South Dakotans or, God forbid, Floridians. Not all of us put our place second. But most do.

Luther Martin charged that Madison & Co. desired "the total abolition and destruction of state governments."[112] Campaign hyperbole? Well, Madison had proposed that the national government "have a negative, in all cases whatsoever, on the Legislative acts of the States." This would have reduced the states to nullities. Madison did not get his way, for which we may be thankful, but 225 years later, when we see the archons of the Federal City effectively overturning a California law legalizing medical marijuana or a New York law setting the drinking age at eighteen, I'm not so sure that Madison didn't have his way after all.

Virginia had vanquished New Jersey, but Martin conceded nothing. On June 20, he dragged the assembly back to first principles. "At the separation from the British Empire," he said via Madison's account, "the people of America preferred the establishment of themselves into thirteen separate sovereignties instead of incorporating themselves into one."[113] Here we pick him up in Yates, who, as usual, channels Martin with much greater force. He concedes that "Congress ought to have been invested with more extensive powers" under the Articles, but the states were rightly jealous of infringements upon their sovereignty. "The time is now come," grants Martin, "to modify" the Articles, but "the grant [of additional power] is a State grant." The states preceded the union, and they cannot be swallowed by it. "[I]f the one was incompatible with the other, I would support the State government at the expense of the Union."[114]

A week later came the rambling, Castro-length, three-hour speech of June 27 that forever fixed Luther Martin's reputation as Bore Nonpareil. Madison in his notes gives a terse and snippy summary of the talk, editorializing that Martin "contended at great length and with great eagerness" that, among other things, the powers of government "ought to be kept within narrow limits," "that an equal vote in each State was essential to the federal idea," "that the States, particularly the smaller, would never allow a negative to be exercised over their laws," and so on, until, exhausted, he sat down only to rise up on the morrow, like some unforgivably chatty and indefatigable houseguest, and discourse, diffusely and vehemently, on the idea that "the General Government ought to be formed for the States, not for individuals."[115]

Yates is a rather more careful amanuensis than Madison, at least when it comes to recording Martin's June 27–28 disquisition. He does, however, preface his transcription in this way: "As [Martin's] arguments were too diffuse, and in many instances desultory, it was not possible to trace him through the whole, or to methodize his ideas into a systematic or argumentative arrangement." Fair enough. Martin, even his champions (if they be plural) must concede, spoke diffusely. Not to mention profusely.

But what did he say? Martin, via Yates, is coherent. He defends what he regards as true federalism: "States will take care of their internal police and local concerns. The general government has no interest but the protection of the whole. Every other government must fail. We are proceeding in forming this government, as if there were no State governments at all."

He objects to bicameralism, for if states are the fundament of the order, and each state has an equal vote, there is no need for a second house.

"The cornerstone of a federal government," says Martin, "is equality of votes." If representation is apportioned on the basis of population, King Numbers will rule. The largest states, in concert, may dictate to their sisters. This, he says, is slavery. Singling out Virginia's insistence upon an inequality of representation, he ends his first day's address with this line, quoted by Yates but ignored by Madison of Virginia: "What are called human feelings in this instance, are only the feelings of ambition and the lust of power."[116] That one hit a little too close to home to take down, James?

Refreshed, Martin returns to the hall on Thursday, June 28, to finish his speech. The Federalists groan.

In Lansing's notes, which were not published until 1939, Martin's remarks are presented tersely and with the periods that Madison disdained to give them. (Madison enhances Martin's verbosity by connecting his transcribed points with semicolons rather than giving them room to breathe with the use of periods.) But the gist of his two-day discourse is not appreciably different: Lansing's Martin insists that the "general Government [is] only intended to protect State Governments," and that "National Objects for Legislative and Executive Exertion ought to be defined and much contracted." If the modest revisions he foresees are inadequate to the task, then a "future Convention" can fix the defects.

"Experience shews the Genius of People is in Favor of small Governments," says Martin, and "they are for seperating [sic] whenever they are remote from its Seat." A national empire of the sort embedded in the Virginia plan would fall apart—deservedly so.

On the second day of the "lengthy harangue," in Farrand's phrase, Martin delivers a lovely line that Lansing records but Madison does not: "Happiness is preferable to the Splendors of a national Government."[117]

Happiness. A Jefferson word. And used in this instance as antonymic to splendor. Martin was speaking on behalf of American modesty, which is perhaps why publicists for the American empire find this particular Founder so useless.

Luther Martin spoke fifty-three times in the convention, far less than, say, Madison or James Wilson. Only a handful of these were more than motions, seconds, or "brief observations." But he who takes the minutes delivers the judgment of the ages. Luther Martin was encased forever in the Independence Hall diorama as diffusely vehement, or vehemently diffuse. Best for posterity to simply ignore what he said.

Even the sympathetic biographer, however, must admit that the evidence of Martin's tediousness is impressive, if not overwhelming. Supreme Court Justice Roger B. Taney, in his memoirs (1872), would recall that while Martin was "a profound lawyer," he committed the sin of non-omission. He never left anything out. As a result, "he was not always listened to. He introduced so much extraneous matter, or dwelt so long on unimportant points, that the attention was apt to be fatigued and withdrawn, and the logic and force of his argument lost upon the Court or the jury."[118]

Taney reports that Martin "often appeared in Court evidently intoxicated,"[119] and the question naturally occurs: Was Martin drunk in Philadelphia, too? Was his a dipso soliloquy?

Contemporaneous accounts offer little evidence. Certainly his postconvention poison-pen pal Oliver Ellsworth would not have scrupled to mention Martin's inebriation if such had been the case. Or maybe, as the wisecrack goes, you'd never know he was a drunk unless you saw him sober.

In any event, Martin's two-day stemwinder struck a nerve. Madison and Wilson rose to refute him, the former dismissing fears of a large-state bloc in a proportional-representation Congress by denying a "common interest" shared by Virginia, Massachusetts, and Pennsylvania. (Time proved Madison correct: the big states never did gang up on their smaller brethren.) Madison also emphasized that the national government's negative on "State laws, will make it an essential branch of the State Legislatures"— cold comfort to those not in the nationalist camp.[120]

The row even woke up Doctor Franklin. Gave him religion, in fact: Franklin, sensing perhaps that Martin's hard-core confederalist position had more support within the hall than it really did, suggested "humbly applying to the Father of lights to illuminate our understandings."

Waxing philosophical, the old deist told his juniors that "the longer I live, the more convincing proofs I see of this truth—*that God Governs in the affairs of men*. And if a sparrow cannot fall to the ground without his notice, is it probable that an empire can rise without his aid?"

Mr. Martin, the noisy fly plashing about in the ointment, did not want an empire to rise. He favored only a modest confederation—not beneath notice from the God who Governs, surely, but not in need of any strenuous cornerstone-laying, either. The structure—the Articles—was already there. In any case, Hamilton smoothly swept Franklin's motion aside with the observation that calling in a clergyman would alert the curious citizenry outside that all was not well. Hugh Williamson of North Carolina added, with more candor, that "The Convention had no funds" anyway.[121]

Martin understood quite clearly that the Constitution was a counterrevolution, recentralizing that which had been decentralized upon the assertion of American independence. "Men love power," Hamilton told the convention.[122] To Hamilton this was a simple statement of fact, not at all deplorable. The Anti-Federalists had their doubts about its accuracy—did not men love their families, their homeplaces, their liberties even more?—but in the event, they desired not to channel this powerlust toward profitable ends but rather to block those avenues down which power is pursued. If it is true that men love to wield power over other men and that a centralized state will attract such warped creatures, then rather than design a Rube Goldberg scheme by which the will to dominate is transmuted into gold for the commonweal, why not just *not* construct a centralized state? Remove the means of gratifying the temptation.

Luther Martin was "the bitterest states' rightser at the Convention," wrote Christopher and James Lincoln Collier. "He was unyielding, beyond compromise on the point, and when he spoke on the issue it was always in the strongest of terms."[123] This is because he conned the game and he kenned the consequences. Not only the rights of the states but their very existence was at stake.

Lest the dire warnings of Martin and the Anti-Federalists be dismissed as so much alarmist hokum, consider that not every nationalizer spoke with politic caution. Delaware's George Read declared: "Too much attachment is betrayed to the State Governments. We must look beyond their continuance. A national Govt. must soon of necessity swallow all of them up. They will soon be reduced to the mere office of electing the national Senate."[124] Effused Read: We must "do . . . away States altogether."[125]

Or ponder the exchange between James Wilson, the archcentralist Scotsman, and Alexander Hamilton. Though putatively representing Pennsylvania and New York, their ultimate loyalties could never be centered upon mere states of a confederacy.

"With me, it is not a desirable object to annihilate the State governments," Wilson said on June 19, "and here I differ from the honorable gentleman from New York. In all extensive empires, a subdivision of power is necessary."

Hamilton objected, ever so mildly, to Wilson's verb. In his lengthy address of the day ultimo, "my meaning was, that a national government ought to be able to support itself without the aid or interference of the state governments," explained Hamilton. The states, he added, "will be dangerous to the national government, and ought to be extinguished, new modified, or reduced to a smaller scale."[126]

Extinguish, yes; annihilate, no. The only difference is in the violence of the verb.

Hamilton and Wilson were the most prominent recent immigrants at the convention. Predictably, they were the most doctrinaire nationalists. Neither had ties to any particular postage stamp of American ground, so their loyalties were not intensely local but rather abstractly national. Wilson, the philosophical champion of centralization, was a land speculator who did not arrive in this country until he was twenty-two years of age. And as Catherine Drinker Bowen writes of Hamilton, "He felt no loyalty to New

York, did not know the meaning of state pride, was not born to it and looked on it as stupid provinciality."[127]

There were many such gusts of universalist wind blowing down Federalist Row. One Hartford promoter of the Constitution exalted "those whose views are not bounded by the town or country which they may represent, not by the state in which they reside, nor even by the union—their philanthropy embraces the interests of all nations."[128]

Henry Knox, who would serve as Washington's secretary of war, wrote Rufus King in July 1787: "The state systems are the accursed things which will prevent our being a nation. . . . [T]he vile State governments are sources of pollution which will contaminate the American name for ages. . . . Smite them, in the name of God and the people."[129]

Certain Federalists made a virtue of rootlessness. Gouverneur Morris played this theme on July 5: "He came here as a Representative of America," wrote Madison; yea, "he flattered himself he came here in some degree as a Representative of the whole human race; for the whole human race will be affected by the proceedings of this Convention." Having struck a note of universalist grandiosity, Morris urged his fellow delegates to go "beyond the narrow limits of place from which they derive their political origin." Place, it seems, was an anchor. Not a mooring, a gift of fixity, but rather the kind of anchor that drags one down, that burdens and ultimately sinks the intellect and the finer qualities.

"State attachments," declared Morris, "and State importance have been the bane of this Country."

"We cannot annihilate" the States, he admitted—alas!—"but we may perhaps take out the teeth of the serpents." Hail the Constitution as defanger!

To hell with place, with locality, with preferment for one's home. Morris concluded by wishing "our ideas to be enlarged to the true interest of man, instead of being circumscribed within the narrow compass of a particular Spot." Sounding like a twenty-first-century globalist, he asked, "Who can say whether he himself, much less whether his children, will the next year be an inhabitant of this or that State[?]"[130] Behold: the Founder as IBM recruiter!

By late June, tempers, like the temperature, boiled. Threats became less veiled. Frankness and sharp exchanges replaced the early cordiality. "[W]e were on the verge of dissolution," Martin wrote later, "scarce held together by the strength of an hair."[131]

Alexander Hamilton, on June 29, dismissed Martin's recent address as plainly contrary to facts. The nationalists pushed ahead. William Pierce, the Georgian whose sometimes catty assessments would pierce the posthumous reputations of delegates who took the other side, insisted that "State distinctions must be sacrificed as far as the general good required."[132] He was here as a Georgian, he said, measuring himself for a marble robe, but "I consider myself a citizen of the United States, whose general interest I will always support."[133]

Oliver Ellsworth of Connecticut moved that each state have an equal vote in the Senate. Madison and Wilson pounced. The latter raised the specter of disunion, proclaiming manfully that if the union be torn asunder by the selfishness of the small states, "it would neither stagger his sentiments nor his duty."[134]

Franklin roused himself to complain that "The smaller States, by this motion, would have the power of giving away the money of the greater States."[135] He offered his own motion, which may kindly be described as impractical, tying suffrage to revenues. It was politely ignored.

Against the big guns of Federalism, Luther Martin replied with uncharacteristic pithiness: "If we cannot confederate on just principles, I will never confederate in any other manner."[136]

Late on Saturday, June 30, Delaware's Gunning Bedford delivered an impolitic warning on behalf of the diminutive. "The little States are willing to observe their engagements," said Bedford, "but will meet the large ones on no ground but that of the Confederation. We have been told with a dictatorial air that this is the last moment for a fair trial in favor of a good Government. . . . The Large States dare not dissolve the Confederation. If they do the small ones will find some foreign ally of more honor and good faith, who will take them by the hand and do them justice."

An exceedingly unwise remark it was, and Rufus King of Massachusetts immediately rebuked Bedford for his "intemperance." King was "grieved that such a thought had entered into his heart," and even "more grieved that such an expression had dropped from his lips." To "court relief from a foreign power" was treasonous and unmanly.[137] (Five days later Bedford took the floor to issue an apology of sorts, claiming that he had been "misunderstood," but rephrasing his warning that "no man can foresee to what extremities the small States may be driven by oppression.")

The efficacy of threats and veiled hints of violence are not often admitted, but the plain fact is that they sometimes work. Bedford's blurt, like the hangman's noose, concentrated minds. By giving disunion a voice he may well have promoted union. And besides, Bedford was positively circumspect in comparison with the bludgeon Gouverneur Morris used on July 5: "This Country must be united. If persuasion does not unite it, the sword will. . . . The scenes of horror attending civil commotion can not be described, and the conclusion of them will be worse than the term of their continuance. The stronger party will then make traytors of the weaker; and the Gallows & Halter will finish the work of the sword."[138]

This from the randy little peg leg who represented the entire human race! Like so many cosmopolitan humanitarians, Morris was willing to put gallows and halter to use in the service of the greater good.

Martin was an ally of the small states but he had far bigger fish to fry, or whales to kill, than finding the best method of apportioning Senate seats. Hell, he was a unicameralist anyway. The battle between large and small states, though it usually emerges as the central story of the convention, Luther Martin viewed as a sidelight. Greater principles were at stake. And Martin, whether windbag or sage, fought it out on the main line.

Tardiness, perhaps as much as avarice and lust, plays its own part in human history. On Monday, July 2, the states split, five to five, on Oliver Ellsworth's motion for an equality of suffrage in the Senate. The tie came as a surprise. Daniel of St. Thomas Jenifer was late to the floor, so Martin, the sole Marylander present, cast his state's vote with Ellsworth. Jenifer arrived immediately thereafter, whereupon Rufus King asked that the question be called again. But you snooze, you lose; a revote would have caused a revolt. (Georgia, too, was divided, only because the sketch artist Pierce had gone to New York to fight a duel.)

General Pinckney of South Carolina, perhaps the only supporter of Franklin's complicated compromise, proposed that a select committee consisting of one member from each state take up the question of congressional representation. Martin gave no ground: "You must give each State an equal suffrage, or our business is at an end."[139]

James Wilson objected. For if the committee was appointed on equal-suffrage principles, would it not produce a compromise along those same principles? Madison, too, expostulated. "[C]ommittees only delay business," he complained, and this one would be mis-shapen by "the whole force of State prejudices."[140]

Pennsylvania cast the sole vote against equal state representation on the committee. Members were chosen by ballot. Luther Martin was Maryland's man—a critical selection, as was Abraham Baldwin of Georgia, a Connecticut native more sympathetic to Middle Atlantic concerns than the other Georgians.

The fix was in. Working from a new compromise suggested by the conciliatory Dr. Franklin, the select committee proposed on July 5 that in the first branch each state should have one representative for every 40,000 inhabitants, and that in the second branch each state should have an equal vote. All bills for raising or appropriating money were to originate in the first branch, and the second had not the power to alter or amend these. (Martin objected to this as another slap at the states, whose interests senators were supposed to represent.)

Presenting this cobblement to the convention, Elbridge Gerry and George Mason tendered the olive branches. Though large-state men, they sought to accommodate their small-state brethren.

The ultranationalists fumed. Hilariously, James Wilson huffed that "the Committee had exceeded their powers."[141] As if the convention had not already done so, in spades!

Madison, too, belittled the compromise. Stick to proportional representation and let the chips, or little states, fall where they may, he said. Surely Delaware and other such trifles would choose submission to their sister states over a foreign alliance. (Madison's strictures are the last comments recorded by Yates, who, with Lansing, saw the writing on the wall and hied off.)

If Wilson and Madison spurned their half a loaf, Martin scorned his with don't-tread-on-me defiance. He had supported the compromise in committee only because it was better than the Virginia Plan; he reserved the right to give a "solemn dissent" should the final product be "inconsistent with the freedom and happiness" of his country.[142] He did, and it was.

For small states to accept equality only in the Senate, said Martin, was like "consenting, after they had struggled, to put both their feet on our necks, to take one of them off, provided we would consent to let them keep the other on; when they knew at the same time, that they could not put one foot on our necks, unless we would consent to it."[143] Martin suspected that in time, the basis of representation in the Senate would be shifted—a suspicion not borne out. The compromise has held for 220 years and counting.

In a confederation, the states are considered as individuals, argued Martin. Just as within a state "one man ought not to have more votes than another, because he is wiser, stronger, or wealthier," so should one state within a confederation not have more votes than its weaker, poorer, or less populous neighbor. In the state of nature, waxed Martin in a Lockean vein that was surely recognizable to his Federalist opponents, each man is "equally free and equally independent."[144] So, too (and much more plausibly), is each state before it enters a confederation.

Was this to be a unitary government acting upon four million individuals? Or was it a confederation of thirteen states, "thirteen distinct political individual existences"? If the former, then an equality of state suffrage in either house of Congress was an offense, as it elevated the individual who happened to reside in

Maryland over the individual who happened to reside in Virginia. But if the latter, then equality of state suffrage ought to be the rule in both houses. In fact, the second house becomes a duplication without purpose. A unicameral legislature would do—as Martin contended, with Paterson and perhaps Franklin, against the tide.

Small-state partisans challenged the delegates of the Big Three to name a single instance under the Articles "where a bad measure had been adopted, or a good measure had failed of adoption, in consequence of the States having an equal vote."[145] There were hems and haws but no adducement of laws.

The Great Compromise of July 16, 1787, by which the convention agreed, five states to four, Wilson and Madison feverishly objecting, to an equality of representation in the Senate is hailed as wisdom itself, though it amounts, really, to no more than splitting the difference between the small states and large. The federal principle was preserved in the Senate; the House, its seats apportioned by population (including fractional representation of slaves), was set on the twin pillars of democratic equality (a Virginian counted for as much as a Delawarean) and nationalism (for the central state was assumed to be in direct relation with the individual rather than with the thirteen states).

Martin voted aye. "He was willing," Madison records him, "to make trial of the plan, rather than do nothing." James Wilson complained that the large states were getting the shaft, and Martin called his bluff: "He was for letting a separation take place if they desired it. He had rather there should be two Confederacies, than one founded on any other principle than an equality of votes in the 2nd branch at least."[146]

The next day, July 17, was another go-round of Madison v. Martin. Score this one for the man from Maryland—sort of.

If Martin is, now and then, reluctantly given credit for standing (or swaying and staggering, depending on the hour) on principle, his critics more often mock him for what is said to be his inadvertent parentage of the clause in Article VI declaring "This constitution, and the laws of the United States which shall be made in pursuance thereof; and all treaties made, or which shall be made, under the authority of the United States, shall be the supreme law of the land; and the judges in every state shall be bound thereby, any thing in the constitution or laws of any state to the contrary notwithstanding."

Hah! his detractors fleer. This was among Martin's scarce "positive virtues" and it was, quite obviously, a mistake.[147] The states' rights man had undermined his own cause with the supremacy clause.

Or maybe not. For one thing, Martin's motion of July 17, borrowed from the New Jersey Plan, was phrased less tautly than the language that was written into the Constitution. Martin's motion read: "that the Legislative acts of the U.S. made by virtue & in pursuance of the articles of Union, and all Treaties made & ratified under the authority of the U.S. shall be the supreme law of the respective States, as far as those acts or treaties shall relate to the said States, or their Citizens and inhabitants—& that the Judiciaries of the several States shall be bound thereby in their decisions, any thing in the respective laws of the individual States to the contrary notwithstanding."[148] This was approved nem con—without dissent—but rewritten such that Martin would denounce the final clause as "worse than useless."[149] He had not envisioned inferior federal courts, for one thing, which "would eventually absorb and swallow up the State judiciaries,"[150] nor had he wanted to subjugate state constitutions to the national document. His intention, he said, was that treaties and general laws would first be subject to the approval of "the courts of the respective states,"[151] an interpretation banished from the revision. For as Patrick Henry said in condemning this clause during the Virginia ratifying convention, "The laws of Congress being paramount to those of the states, and to their constitutions also, whenever they come in competition, the judges must decide in favor of the former."[152]

But Martin's "supreme law" motion can also be seen—and almost certainly was conceived—as a federalist alternative to the single most nationalist aspect of the Virginia Plan.

Immediately antecedent to Martin's July 17 motion, the convention had considered granting the national government the power "to negative all laws passed by the several States contravening in the opinion of the National Legislature the articles of Union, or any treaties subsisting under the authority of the Union."

This extraordinary negative, which would render the states little more than the picturesque titles assigned different tourist regions, was spoken for only by its progenitor and most ardent advocate: James Madison. By his own notes, Madison "considered the negative on the laws of the States as essential to the efficacy & security of the General Government." Given free rein, the states would "pursue their particular interests in opposition to the general interest." This diversity was to be squelched; the "general interest"—an almost Rousseauian formulation—demanded uniformity. "Nothing short of a negative on their laws will controul [sic]" the obstreperous states.

Oddly, for a republican, Madison evidenced the British Empire: "Nothing could maintain the harmony & subordination of the various parts of the empire, but the prerogative by which the Crown, stifles in the birth every Act of every part tending to discord or encroachment."[153] (As Martin sighed, "we were eternally troubled with arguments and precedents from the British government.")[154]

Madison's enthusiasm for the national negative was too much even for Gouverneur Morris, who thought that "it would disgust all the States."[155] Charles Hobson, editor of the Madison papers, notes that "Madison scholars" and chroniclers of the convention have overlooked Little Jemmy's avid and persistent support of the negative, which "occupied a central place in his plan for extending the sphere of republican government." Monarchism aside, "Madison was scarcely less a consolidationist than Alexander Hamilton," writes Hobson.[156] And with the negative (which Jefferson had condemned in correspondence with Madison), he had found the rod with which to bring the refractory states to heel. It was utterly impractical—"Shall all the laws of the States be sent up to the General Legislature before they shall be permitted to operate?" asked Luther Martin—but Madison's strong suit was theory, not practice.[157]

Madison's ally Charles Pinckney had moved on June 8 to extend the negative to "all laws which [the National Legislature] should judge to be improper." Madison had seconded the motion as "absolutely necessary to a perfect system."[158] A perfect tyranny, perhaps. Without Luther Martin in the hall, the critic's role in early June was assumed by Gunning Bedford of Delaware, who branded the negative a weapon by which the large states would crush the small. As if to confirm Bedford, only Pennsylvania, Massachusetts, and Virginia (with George Mason and Edmund Randolph voting no) cast affirmative votes.

On July 17, in the single greatest triumph for a decentralized republic during that scorching Philadelphia summer, the delegates voted to strike even the modified negative by seven states to three. Two-thirds of the supporters of Madison's negative were the states of Virginia and Massachusetts, which lends colorability to the fear of the small states that their stout brethren would happily oppress them if they could. (The other vote came from North Carolina.)

Madison refused to let the matter rest; he would support a last-ditch attempt by Pinckney on August 23 to grant Congress power to veto state laws by a two-thirds vote in each house. It failed, fortunately for its sponsors, for the state conventions would have rejected a Constitution with such a heavy-handed provision.

Writing Edmund Randolph, Madison instanced state issuance of paper money as the kind of irresponsible local hell-raising that would be snuffed by a national negative. Yet Article 1, Section 10, providing that "No state shall . . . coin money" or "emit bills of credit," did the trick more directly.

Luther Martin's defense of the right of Maryland and other states to print their own currency can be read several ways: as a populist championing of debtors; as a hack's favor to wealthy Maryland speculators; or as an example of a thoughtful man hewing to decentralist principles. The bases for the first two interpretations are shaky, which has not sparked a rush by celebrators of the Miracle at Philadelphia to embrace the third possibility.

Charles Beard, in *An Economic Interpretation of the Constitution of the United States* (1913), ignores Martin's holdings in confiscated Loyalist property and credits his "bitter" opposition to the Constitution to his "sympathy with poor debtors."[159] Martin is one of many exceptions that pockmark the Beardian thesis that merchants, creditors, and holders of public securities formed a fairly solid class in favor of the new Constitution, which would guarantee their properties. For Martin had substantial holdings in public securities ($3,060.67, by Beard's count), thus fitting the profile of the self-interested backer of the Constitution. Forrest McDonald, refuter of Beard, estimates Martin's public security holdings at $4,400, making him the eighteenth-largest holder of such among the delegates. The cold calculus of wealth-maximization ought to have placed him with Wilson and Madison. The other Anti-Federalist in the Maryland delegation, John Francis Mercer, also owned public securities. But man does not vote by holdings alone. Much as I respect Beard the fearless iconoclast, the unsatisfying tenuity of the debtor/Anti-Federalist connection does a disservice to the breadth of Martin's articulation of the decentralist alternative to Madison-Wilson nationalism. Luther Martin was cast in no easily recognizable mold; he fit no pigeonhole.

The Constitution-makers never did credit the scattered recusants with insight, ability, or even good faith. Their motives were impugned, their attachments questioned. Elbridge Gerry, for instance, was dismissed as a "Grumbletonian."[160] On July 10, George Washington wrote the absent Alexander Hamilton: "The Men who oppose a strong & energetic government are, in my opinion, narrow minded politicians, or are under the influence of local views."[161] The possibility that they were acting from a legitimate fear of centralization or a principled belief in the merits of confederacy seems not to have occurred to Madison, Wilson, Hamilton, and Washington. Only the stupid, the disloyal, and the corrupt would stand in the way of progress.

The convention adjourned on July 25; two days later Martin left for a week in Baltimore, returning August 4. On the 6th he noticed his Maryland colleague McHenry holding a list of delegate names that were marked "for" or "against." McHenry had obtained the list from Mercer, who said that he had recorded the position of delegates on whether or not to install an American king.[162] More than twenty were marked as favoring monarchy. Mercer would later deny that he had told McHenry that these men were monarchists.

Martin, upon returning home postconvention, would make use of the list in his "Tavern harangues."[163] For his part, McHenry wrote Daniel Carroll on January 9, 1788, that "Nothing that Mr. Martin can say can make me uneasy, or give me any Surprize [sic]."[164]

Martin, Mercer, and McHenry may have misunderstood each other. Or maybe not. Gordon Wood writes that "we shall never understand events of the 1790s until we take seriously, as contemporaries did, the possibility of some sort of monarchy's developing in America."[165] It was something more than chimerical. Martin saw through the Hamiltonian scrim, and he was uncouth enough to say what he saw.

Martin left for New York on August 7, the day after the Committee of Detail, from which Martin was excluded, had presented its collated articles of the draft constitution. He returned on the 13th. From mid-August until his departure in early September, Martin met nightly with Gerry, Mason, and assorted disgruntled delegates. Forrest McDonald, in his richly rewarding *E Pluribus Unum: The Formation of the American Republic, 1776–1790* (1965), calls them "watered-down old republicans," each with a "personal or economic axe to grind,"[166] but a more charitable reading might fix them as allies thrown together, willy-nilly, on the federalist side of a centralizing equation. They were about to be crushed and they knew it, so in fellowship and strong drink they passed the eves of late August, talking strategy, grumbling about the victors, and wondering what would come next. Martin and Mercer would leave; Gerry and Mason would fight it out on the main line and then refuse to sign on the bottom line; others of this club (Randolph, Charles Pinckney) pursued idiosyncratic courses.

The Constitution faced obstacles yet—particularly whether a supermajority was necessary to pass navigation, or tariff, acts—but the end was drawing near.

Martin and his oft-reviled colleague Gerry upheld the flag of antimilitarism at the convention. On August 18, the duo proposed to limit the size of the standing army in peacetime. (The precise limit to be determined later: Gerry suggested two or three thousand.)

Gerry, who in the accounts of court historians would come off as something of a boob, a silly man quite incapable of the task at hand, expressed surprise that "there was no check here against standing armies in time of peace." In Madison's account, "He thought an army dangerous in time of peace & could never consent to a power to keep up an indefinite number."[167] Gerry and Martin then made their motion, which failed to attract the vote of a single state.

(Madison did apprehend the danger of standing armies, even as posterity has not. He said on June 29, "In time of actual war, great discretionary powers are constantly given to the Executive Magistrate. Constant apprehension of war, has the same tendency to render the head too large for the body. A standing military force, with an overgrown Executive will not long be safe companions to liberty. The means of defence against foreign danger, have been always the instruments of tyranny at home."[168] Do not expect these words ever to be quoted in a U.S. Department of Education Constitution syllabus.)

"Martin was confident that the States would never give up the power over the Militia," Madison records on August 23.[169] Well, they did and they didn't. State militias were effectively nationalized through the National Guard, though in recent years feisty states such as Massachusetts and Minnesota have fought—unsuccessfully—to prevent their National Guard units from being shipped out of the country to fight the Empire's wars.

Time and again, Luther Martin stood alone, or nearly so, in attempting to infuse the new Constitution with something of the spirit of '76. He was a libertarian in a body of men convinced that America needed a more vigorous government; he spoke of decentralism to men with centripetal convictions. He might not be seconded; oft he was rebuffed, rebutted, reproached. But he kept on coming.

Thrice he proposed to bar the president from reelection. He advocated the appointment of judges by the Senate, not the executive. (Madison conceded that concurrence of the second branch might guard against "any incautious or corrupt nomination by the Executive."[170] Martin got half of this loaf.) He called for senators to be paid by the states, not the national government, because "the Senate is to represent the States, [so] the members of it ought to be paid by the States."[171] He successfully proposed to affix "or on confession in open court" to the requirement that "No person be convicted of treason unless on the testimony of two witnesses to the same overt act."[172] (He would revisit the grounds for treason much later.) Martin moved that the Electoral Collegians be chosen by state legislatures. His was the only stated objection to (and Maryland's the only vote against) per-capita voting by senators. He wished them to vote as a unit by states, in keeping with the gist of the Articles. He successfully opposed a clause, proposed by Charles Pinckney and Gouverneur Morris, that would give the national government the power "to subdue a rebellion in any State" even if the legislature of the state had not requested intervention.[173]

On August 21, he greeted the morning with a motion, seconded by his colleague McHenry, requiring that direct taxation (which in any event "should not be used but in case of absolute necessity")[174] be paid by the states into the national treasury rather than be levied directly by the national government. It failed, 7–1, with only New Jersey voting aye. (Maryland was divided.)

Later that day, he committed an act of supreme tactlessness, raising the issue that all had tacitly agreed must not be raised: the enshrinement of slavery in the U.S. Constitution. As Charles Warren writes in *The Making of the Constitution* (1929), "Hitherto, the highly inflammable topic of slavery had been touched upon in the debates only from the economic and political standpoints."[175] Luther Martin framed the question another way.

Madison, as is his wont, abridges what must have been an impassioned declamation. Perhaps the subject bored him. Martin proposed to "allow a prohibition or tax on the importation of slaves." He offered reasons both political and moral. First, because a slave is counted as sixth-tenths of a man for purposes of apportionment, the Constitution provides "encouragement" of this vile traffic. Second, "slaves weakened one part of the Union which the other parts were bound to protect." Which raises the question, not answered by Madison's shorthand: which was the weakened part? The section scarce of slaves, which was disadvantaged in divvying up the House of Representatives, or the slave belt, which was morally strangulated? For Martin's third point was that "it was inconsistent with the principles of the revolution and dishonorable to the American character to have such a feature in the Constitution."[176]

This was not the first time the peculiar institution had intruded into Independence Hall. Delegates had wrangled over how to count slaves from July 11–13, and on August 8, Messrs. King and

G. Morris registered their objections to this flagitious trade. In the final document, slaves—or "all other persons," in the Constitution's prissy euphemism—counted as three-fifths of a person in apportioning representation and direct taxes. In recent years the 60 percent clause has achieved a symbolic status—undeservedly so. Were not slaves men and women and deserving of full enumeration? ask the sanctimonious. Well, the matter is hardly black-and-white. It was southern delegates—Charles Pinckney and Pierce Butler of South Carolina—who moved to scrap the three-fifths rule and count blacks "*equally* with the Whites."[177] Martin believed that they ought not to count at all: they were property, in the eyes of the state, mere possessions, "no more than Cattle, Horses, Mules, or Asses,"[178] and in counting them the federal charter was only augmenting the influence of the southern states. (Martin was hardly acting the pinched and narrow parochialist here: Maryland had almost half as many slaves—103,036—as free persons—216,692—according to the 1790 census.)

Martin's characteristically blunt assault on the institution of slavery sparked a debate that would carry over into the next day. Though "debate" is not quite the word, for as usual, Luther was trampled.

John Rutledge of South Carolina spoke in Hamiltonian realpolitikspeak: "Religion & humanity had nothing to do with this question. Interest alone is the governing principle with nations." Oliver Ellsworth of Connecticut, whose postconvention libels were to sully Martin's reputation for generations—nay, centuries!—for once took up the position that "the States are the best judges of their particular interest," at least when it comes to importing African bondsmen. "Let us not intermeddle," he said, contrary to his inclinations. His Nutmeg State confrère, Roger Sherman, thought it best to leave well enough alone—"to leave the matter as we find it." The states, he predicted, would abolish slavery on their own. Charles Pinckney—"Constitution Charley," as he was mockingly called in later years, when he lied about his age to make the false claim that he was the youngest delegate at the convention—declared flatly that if the slave trade were forbidden, South Carolina was out. Besides, added his second cousin, Charles Cotesworth Pinckney, servitude boosted the GNP: "The more slaves, the more produce to employ the carrying trade; The more consumption also, and the more of this, the more of revenue for the common treasury."

Taking up the cause of the African was Martin's southern neighbor George Mason, who blamed this "infernal traffic" on "the avarice of British Merchants." The slave trade he pronounced an "evil" that had been prohibited by the Virginia and Maryland legislatures. Unless interdicted by the general government, this wickedness would continue through the ports of South Carolina and Georgia. Like Martin, Mason resisted most grants of power to the new government save the one withheld: that of barring, immediately, the import of slaves.

Before Jefferson heard the firebell in the night, George Mason foretold its tolling: "Every master of slaves is born a petty tyrant," he declared. "They bring the judgment of heaven on a Country. As nations can not be rewarded or punished in the next world they must be in this. By an inevitable chain of causes & effects providence punishes national sins, by national calamities."[179] Ours was carried in the stinking holds of ships making the middle passage.

The matter was referred to a committee, and in due course a clause was inserted banning the satanic traffic after 1808. That the document contained any stricture whatsoever upon the slave trade may be credited to Luther Martin.

The ban on the importation of slaves was part of the last great compromise of the convention. On August 24, a Committee of Eleven recommended that Congress (1) have no right to ban the slave trade before 1800 (later delayed until 1808), which propitiated the southern states; and (2) be permitted to pass navigation acts with a simple majority vote instead of the two-thirds stipulated in the draft document.

Martin, reliably, tried to derail this compromise. On August 29, he seconded the motion of Charles Pinckney that acts "regulating the commerce of the U.S. with foreign powers, or among the several States" required the approval of two-thirds of each house of Congress. Pinckney's motion, which would have effectively eliminated high tariffs and made the U.S. a kind of free-trade zone, failed, attracting only the votes of Maryland, Virginia, North Carolina, and Georgia.

Also on the 29th, Martin asserted, vainly, the position of the "limited States" against "the large States" on the matter of the disposition of western lands. The sudden embrace of state territorial integrity by the likes of G. Morris and James Wilson amused him: "He wished," Madison transcribed Martin as saying, that "Mr. Wilson had thought a little sooner of the value of *political* bodies. In the beginning, when the rights of the small States were in question, they were phantoms, ideal beings. Now when the Great States were to be affected, political societies were of a sacred nature."

Why should the people of the western lands not have the right to form their own states? And why must Maryland and New Jersey and Delaware "guarantee the Western claims of the large" states?[180] This dispute was a carryover from the debate over the Articles. It felt stale.

Summer's end was in the air. It was a time for summing up. On August 31, George Mason said that he would "sooner chop off his right hand than put it to the Constitution as it now stands,"[181] and in the end, he did neither. "There is no declaration of rights," he later said by way of explaining his refusal to sign the document. "There is no declaration of any kind for preserving the liberty of the press, the trial by jury in civil cases, nor the danger of standing armies in time of peace."

Mason's objections were sweeping and took in all three branches of the new government. The House of Representatives would provide "the shadow only" and not the substance of real representation. The Senate, with its powers of appointment and treaty-making and its elongated six-year terms, "will destroy any balance in government." As for the federal judiciary, it is "so constructed and extended as to absorb and destroy the judiciaries of the several states." In transferring the administration of justice to a remote capital, it renders "justice as unattainable" and enables "the rich to oppress and ruin the poor."

The executive, without benefit of a constitutional council chosen by the states through the House of Representatives, will be "directed by minions and favorites." His helpmeet, "that unnecessary officer, the Vice-President . . . for want of other employment, is made president of the Senate; thereby dangerously blending the executive and legislative powers."

A very bad moon was on the rise. "This government," predicted Mason, "will commence in a moderate aristocracy: it is at present impossible to foresee whether it will, in its operation, produce a monarchy or a corrupt oppressive aristocracy; it will most probably vibrate some years between the two, and then terminate in the one or the other."[182]

(We have no need of simple morality plays here. If by common assessment Martin and Mason were the closest thing to libertarians in Philadelphia, Mason nevertheless proposed on August 20 to enable Congress "to enact sumptuary laws" regulating, inter alia, eating, drinking, clothing, and manners.[183] For his part, Martin objected to the Constitution's ban on religious tests, coyly remarking that "there were some members so unfashionable as to think, that a belief of the existence of a Deity, and of a state of future rewards and punishments would be some security for the good conduct of our rulers." Besides, "in a Christian country, it would be at least decent to hold out some distinction between the professors of Christianity and downright infidelity or paganism."[184] You can almost see his farouche snarl directed Monticello way.)

Never afraid to stand alone, Martin moved on August 31 that the approval of all thirteen states be required for ratification. He lost, nine states to one. He and Daniel Carroll, over Jenifer's dissent, cast the only state vote against final passage of the ratification clause. Nine states only would be necessary to junk the Articles and get this party started. Martin later explained that

> It was my opinion, that to agree upon a ratification of the constitution by any less number than the whole thirteen states, is so directly repugnant to our present articles of confederation, and the mode therein prescribed for their alteration, and such a violation of the compact which the states, in the most solemn manner, have entered into with each other, that those who could advocate a contrary proposition, ought never to be confided in, and entrusted in public life.[185]

Martin and Carroll also caused Maryland to cast the sole vote against ratification by convention, Martin contending that state legislatures were the proper arbitrators. Martin was no mobocrat. In his brief remarks on state conventions we can foresee the Federalist of 1800 in utero. He understood "the danger of commotions from a resort to the people,"[186] for the people can be gulled, the people fall for lies, the people can rampage. Martin was an Anti-Federalist but he was not a populist. Nor, however, was he a preening aristocrat. Within the convention, he stood at antipodes from the likes of Hamilton or the silly liar-about-his-age Charles Pinckney, who suggested property qualifications of $100,000 for president and $50,000 for senators, representatives, and federal judges. (Doctor Franklin piped up that some of the greatest rogues were the richest rogues, and Pinckney's plutocratic motion died.)

Martin left Philadelphia on September 4. He intended, he said, to return, but did not. Two weeks of dotting constitutional i's and crossing t's remained, yet despite "two months close application under those august and enlightened masters of the science with which the Convention abounded," Martin had been unable to discover "anything in the history of mankind . . . to warrant or countenance the motley mixture of a system proposed." The Constitution

> was neither wholly federal, nor wholly national—but a strange hotch-potch of both—just so much federal in appearance as to give its advocates . . . an opportunity of passing it as such upon the unsuspecting multitude, before they had time and opportunity to examine it, and yet so predominantly national as to put it in the power of its movers, whenever the machine shall be set agoing, to strike out every part that has the appearance of being federal, and to render it wholly and entirely a national government.[187]

The opposition lacked bodies. Not only Sam Adams and Willie Jones, George Clinton and Patrick Henry. It wanted Shaysites. Agrarians. Sons of liberty. As Clinton Rossiter admitted, "If a dozen spokesmen of [liberty and localism] had shown up in Philadelphia and then stuck to their guns, it is hard to see how Madison and his friends could have pieced together a nationalist charter."[188]

Had Martin remained till the bitter end, he would have joined Elbridge Gerry, George Mason, and Edmund Randolph in refusing to sign the engrossed Constitution on September 17. The vacillatory Randolph hadn't been much of an ally to Martin, Lansing, and Yates, the Anti-Federalist hardcore. Nor had the two most famous non-signers, Mason and Gerry, voted with the Middle Atlantic "true federalist" bloc. As Martin observed, "the first of those gentlemen could not forget he belonged to the *Ancient Dominion*, nor could the latter forget, that he represented Old Massachusetts." But as they came to realize that the Madisonian octopus would choke the states, even Virginia and Massachusetts, Mason and Gerry, "being *republicans* and *federalists*," became "warmly and zealously opposed" to the Constitution.[189] (Ironically, Elbridge Gerry, whose name would become the first half of a compound verb meaning to unfairly design election districts, told the Massachusetts legislature that his principal reason for opposing the Constitution was that "there is no adequate provision for a representation of the people.")[190]

One cringes to read the diffident James McHenry of Maryland schlubbishly confessing to the convention on September 17 that although he dislikes "many parts of the system," he will affix his signature because "I distrust my own judgement, especially as it is opposite to the opinion of a majority of gentlemen whose abilities and patriotism are of the first cast; and as I have had already frequent occasions to be convinced that I have not always judged right."[191] The Georgian William Pierce was no model of dispassionate analysis, but his assessment of McHenry is worth quoting: "He is a Man of specious talents, with nothing of genious [sic] to improve them."[192]

Contrast McHenry's unmanly timidity with Luther Martin's forthrightness. Referring to Washington and Franklin, he wrote,

> To find myself under the necessity of opposing such illustrious characters, whom I venerated and loved, filled me with regret; but viewing the system in the light I then did, and yet do view it, to have hesitated would have been criminal; complaisance would have been guilt. If it was the idea of my state that whatever a Washington or Franklin approved, was to be blindly adopted, she ought to have spared herself the expence of sending any members to the Convention.[193]

The last remarks Luther Martin made in Philadelphia were a prediction that Maryland and her sisters "would not ratify" the document "unless hurried into it by surprize."[194] Surely Maryland would stand up for her rights and reject the Constitution.

James McHenry told the story of Martin remarking to Daniel of St. Thomas Jenifer, his fellow Maryland delegate, "I'll be hanged if ever the people of Maryland agree to it." To which Jenifer replied, "I advise you to stay in Philadelphia lest you should be hanged."[195]

Luther Martin went home, and no one would try to hang him. At least, not for another twenty years.

PART TWO

MARYLAND, MY MARYLAND; OR, LUTHER MARTIN'S THESES

THE *Pennsylvania Packet* OF SEPTEMBER 6 PREDICTED: "THE YEAR 1776 is celebrated, says a correspondent, for a revolution in favour of Liberty. The year 1787, it is expected will be celebrated with equal joy for a revolution in favour of Government."[1] Less sanguine was Richard Henry Lee of Virginia, who mourned, "It will be considered, I believe, as a most extraordinary epoch in the history of mankind, that in a few years there should be so essential a change in the minds of men. 'Tis really astonishing that the same people, who have just emerged from a long and cruel war in defence of liberty, should now agree to fix an elective despotism upon themselves and their posterity."[2]

Had the experience of eleven years really soured Americans on liberty? A war for independence had been fought and won under the gentle guidance of loosely bound federation. If the exigencies of the Revolution had not required the centralization of political power, then why was it being forced upon a peaceful and prosperous postwar America? "Who would have thought," marveled New Yorker Melancton Smith, "ten years ago, that the very men, who risked their lives and fortunes in support of republican principles, would now treat them as the fictions of fancy?"[3]

The Articles stipulated that "any alteration . . . be agreed to in a Congress of the United States, and be afterwards confirmed by the legislatures of every State." Unanimity was the rule. But, well, genius recognizes no bounds. Over Maryland's objection, the young Philadelphians ripped up the Articles and instead provided that "The ratification of the conventions of nine States, shall be sufficient for the establishment of this constitution between the States so ratifying the same."

The Congress of the Confederation, as the Continental Congress now styled itself, gave the report of the Philadelphia Convention a consideration barely more than perfunctory before sending it on to the state conventions (not, as the Articles stated, the legislatures) for ratification. Richard Henry Lee, who had been something of a nationalist back in May, even to the point of urging George Mason to support a congressional veto over state laws, called for the Congress to add amendments guaranteeing jury trials, frequent elections, a ban on cruel and unusual punishment, and the freedom of speech, press, assembly, and conscience, but he was unable even to persuade Congress to debate his bill of rights, let alone endorse it.

Lee went into opposition, fearful that the new system would be dominated by "a coalition of monarchy men, military men, aristocrats and drones, whose noise, impudence and zeal exceed all belief."[4] But the Constitution went to the states.

The document sent out to the provinces for ratification was a "misshapened heterogenous monster of ambition and interest,"[5] said Luther Martin, which was hurried through the convention and was being stampeded through the states with a suspicious celerity.

The forces of large-F Federalism pushed for quick action by the states; as with all progressives, deliberation was their enemy. Anti-Federalists asked what was the rush? Did not prudence recommend a careful state-by-state examination of Philadelphia's handiwork? "Federal Farmer" (Melancton Smith) explained of the hurry-up offense that it was "natural for men, who wish to hasten the adoption of a measure, to tell us, now is the crisis—now is the critical moment which must be seized or all will be lost." Don't run with the herd, Federal Farmer pled, for they were headed, as always, to the pen: "The fickle and ardent, in any community, are the proper tools for establishing despotic government."[6]

The Anti-Federalists girded themselves for an epochal debate. The shape of the American nation was on the tapis. What was it to be? A decentralized confederation based on localism and liberty, or a centralized union in which the states were clearly subordinate to a national government endowed with significant powers to tax, override local laws, and make war?

The differences were not found at the margins; the fight was not about the placement of commas. States were being asked to transfer both sword and purse to the federal city. North Carolina Anti-Federalist William Goudy warned that "the last man and the last penny would be extorted from us."[7] The Constitution "will destroy the state governments, whatever may have been the intention," said George Mason. "There are many gentlemen in the United States who think it right that we should have one great, national, consolidated government, and that it was better to bring it about slowly and imperceptibly rather than all at once."[8] Ratify and you will have done their bidding. The coffin will have been carved.

Most Anti-Federalists saw no shades of grey, admitted no ambiguity in this matter. "If it be demonstrated that the adoption of the new plan is a little or a trifling evil," said Patrick Henry, "then, sir, I acknowledge that adoption ought to follow; but, sir, if this be a truth, that its adoption may entail misery on the free people of the country, I then insist that rejection ought to follow."[9]

Kenneth M. Stampp has written that "Only uncertainty about which states would ratify prevented the delegates from writing the preamble to read 'We the People of the States of New Hampshire, Massachusetts, Rhode Island,' etc., rather than 'We the People of the United States.'"[10] The Committee of Detail had delivered unto the convention on August 6 a draft that used just this state-specific formulation. It was the Committee of Style, and its chief penman Gouverneur Morris, which redacted the preamble to read "We the People of the United States." This tectonic shift occurred on September 12, without Luther Martin in the hall to call Morris out for his creative editing.

These first seven preambulary words caused Samuel Adams to stumble at the threshold. Patrick Henry tripped, too, and asked the Virginia ratifying convention. "What right had they to say, *We, the people?* . . . instead of, *We, the states?*"

Upon this difference hung, perhaps, the fate of the country. "States are the characteristics and the soul of a confederation," instructed Henry. "If the states be not the agents of this compact, it must be one great, consolidated, national government, of the people of all the states." So vast a unitary state must, of necessity, be tyrannical. The choice was upon them: "If a wrong step be now made," warned Patrick Henry, "the republic may be lost forever."[11] The game would be up almost before it had begun.

Control the terms used in debate and you control the debate. The consolidationists seized the label "federalist" and stuck the true federalists with an agin' name. This taxonomic legerdemain enraged Luther Martin, who preferred the terms "federal" versus "national," and who noted afterwards that "in convention . . . those who opposed the system were there considered and styled the federal party, those who advocated it, the antifederal."[12] It was all so unfair. To think: a crypto-monarchist like Alexander Hamilton as an author of something called *The Federalist Papers*! Melancton Smith, among the best Anti writers, adopted "Federal Farmer" as his nom de plume, but it was a futile attempt to reclaim the word.

There has been a strain of Constitutionolatry that dismisses the Antis as bitter and indebted farmers and shiftless mechanics, indurated knuckledraggers all, who darkly and unfairly viewed the document as having been framed by aristocrats in the service of the money power. Thus caricatured, they fit easily into the chute that leads down to the memory hole, where dwell forgotten Founders and unheard prophets.

Pulling them out—restoring them to the prominent position they deserve in the American story—is no forlorn hope, no mission perdu. For they left a paper trail. Not *The Federalist Papers*, it is true, but enough Anti-Federalist papers and passages of surpassing eloquence in the state conventions as to make the Antis not only the first noble losers in our history but quite possibly the foremost.

They wrote under such pseudonyms as "Brutus" (Robert Yates), "Centinel" (Samuel Bryan), "Federal Farmer" (Smith), and

"Agrippa" (James Winthrop). They were not carpers or pettifoggers; rather, they laid out the path not traveled, the chance not taken. The Anti-Federalists delineated the American government—or governments, since their central state was weak and preservative of liberty, and real power was scattered throughout the land, as sunflowers in a field—we might have had.

Standing in the front ranks of Anti-Federalist writers is Luther Martin, whose *The Genuine Information,* which has been accurately termed "the ablest argument extant against the fundamental principles of the proposed government,"[13] is *the* Anti-Federalist Paper.

Martin came home from Philadelphia not laden with Sylvester Stallone souvenirs or larded on mounds of inedible cheesesteaks but loaded for bear. He was going to sound the tocsin about what the Philadelphia conspirators had been up to.

The Maryland legislature authorized the printing and distribution of two thousand copies of the Constitution, as well as three hundred copies of a German translation for Teutonophones. The battlefront shifted homewards.

Martin had chafed under the code of secrecy binding the Philadelphia conventioneers. The summer had about it a clandestine quality, as though a cabal were meeting to some nefarious and mysterious purpose. So when, in late November, he and the rest of the Maryland delegation were summoned to Annapolis (all but Mercer appeared) to report on "How I Spent My Summer," he shattered the silence with a—need I even bother with the adjective?—lengthy speech that would appear, serially and revised, between December 28, 1787, and February 8, 1788, in the *Maryland Gazette and Baltimore Advertiser* and then be reprinted under the carnival-barker-esque title *The Genuine Information.* (I shall quote from both speech and pamphlet.)

It was on November 29, 1787, that Luther Martin spoke at arse-shifting length to the Maryland House of Delegates in one of the most powerful, if admittedly diffuse and vehement, assaults ever mounted on the Constitution.

Martin spilled the beans, or at least his version of them. The previous months had seen the occasional pinprick in the bubble of secrecy that had surrounded the convention, but this was a knife slash. He had betrayed confidences in his Annapolis speech, his critics squealed; he had violated the code of silence—a code to which he had never subscribed in any event. Anti-Federalists lauded him. Pennsylvanian Samuel Bryan, writing as "Centinel," was encomiastic:

> He has laid open the conclave, exposed the dark scene within, developed the mystery of the proceedings, and illustrated the machinations of ambition. His public spirit has drawn upon him the rage of the conspirators, for daring to remove the veil of secrecy, and announcing to the public the meditated, gilded mischief: all their powers are exerting for his destruction, the mint of calumny is assiduously engaged in coining scandal to blacken his character, and thereby to invalidate his testimony; but this illustrious patriot will rise superior to all their low arts. . . . [14]

Ah, if only.

Martin's dilation before the Maryland legislature denounced not only the proposed Constitution but the Philadelphia proceedings themselves, which had been conducted with doors locked and paranoia set on orange alert. Communication with the outside world had been barred, "so that we had no opportunity of gaining information by a Correspondence with others."[15]

"I had no idea," said Martin, "that all the wisdom, integrity, and virtue of this State, or of the others, were centered in the convention. . . ."[16]

He hadn't had much time to prepare formal remarks, Martin told the legislators, whose spirits must have risen at the implication of brevity. *Sursum corda*, solons!

But once started, Martin was hard to stop. He had a story to tell.

The Virginians had concocted this damned convention, he said, largely to augment their influence and diminish that of less populous states. Their foremost goal was to obtain a lopsided inequality in suffrage—"as if the want of that was the principal defect in our original system."[17]

Virginia, Pennsylvania, and Massachusetts would dominate this union of unequals. This trio, in control (under the Virginia Plan) of thirteen of the Senate's twenty-eight seats, would have "an undue superiority in making laws and regulations" and "the same superiority in the appointment of the President, the judges, and all other officers of government."[18] This was a coup, plain and simple—a "system of slavery" by which King Numbers bound and gagged the ten virtuous little states.[19] And it was not just any system of slavery. No, this was "the most complete, most abject system of *slavery* that the wit of man ever devised, under the pretence of forming a government for free States."[20] Hyperbole? Sure. But then Luther Martin had seen Alexander Hamilton and James Wilson up close, and he knew the fate of small things in the big dreams of such men.

I don't wish to tarnish any idols, said Martin, but the illustrious Washington and Franklin gave their "hearty concurrence" to this scheme. They were not demigods or paragons of dispassionate judgment but rather fallible men. He did not want to "lessen those exalted characters," assured Martin, "but to show how far the greatest and best of men may be led to adopt very improper measures through error in judgment, State influence, or by other causes." Celebrity is not next to godliness. Let us not "suffer our eyes to be so far dazzled by the splendor of names, as to run blind-folded into what may be our destruction."

Martin strikes here the perfect note: we may reverence the characters of the men who made the Revolution without surren-dering our own critical faculties when considering the political de-cisions they make. He disclaims the role of iconoclast. I venerate these men, says Martin, and am "disposed to pay a deference to their opinions; but I should little have deserved the trust this State reposed in me, if I could have sacrificed its dearest interests to my complaisance for their sentiments."[21]

The malign geniuses behind the convention plotted "the *in-troduction of monarchy*," charged Martin. The king was not to be called king but president, his office "so constituted as to differ from a monarch scarcely but in name."[22] The largest states would have a lock on the office (as they did until 1829). The president's al-most unchecked power to grant "reprieves and pardons" smacked of regal privilege.

Armed with the "absolute negative" over state laws of the Ran-dolph-Madison plan, Virginia would have broken the lesser states to her imperious will. "Such Government would be a Government by Junto and bind hand and foot all the other States in the Union."[23] As it was, the presidential veto supposed that this eminence had "more wisdom or integrity than the senators," a dubious proposition.[24]

The crypto-monarchists acted "covertly," alleged Martin, since the tenor of the times was republican. Their "wish it was to abol-ish and annihilate all State governments, and to bring forward one general government, over this extensive continent, of a monarchical nature, under certain restrictions and limitations." These shrewd dissemblers effected an alliance with a faction that was neither monarchical nor desirous of the abolition of the states but wished only for the aggrandizement of their own states and the consequent minification of others.

The monarchists feared, as a vampire quails at the sight of the cross, "the thirteen State governments, preserved in *full force and energy*." They must efface this gallant baker's dozen without calling down the fury of the people upon their devious heads. So they threw in with that party which favored "giving the government great and undefined powers as to its legislative and executive; well knowing, that, by departing from a federal system, they paved the way for their favorite object, the destruction of the State governments, and the introduction of monarchy."

The third party of the convention, Martin's own, the "truly federal" moderates of the Middle Atlantic, deplored monarchy, despised influence-seeking, and were too modest to assume the role of "master-builders."²⁵ Only the vainglorious would gather in secret conclave to demolish entirely the present union and replace it with a unitary government.

America was young but she had developed habits, old ways that were the best ways. She liked her government close by, unobtrusive but near at hand. She abominated distant capitals. Why, just look at Vermont, at Maine, at the western portions of North Carolina and Virginia and Pennsylvania. Their people wanted states of their own, fashioned by local hands, breathing the local spirit. "[C]an it be supposed," asked Martin, "they would ever submit to have a national government established, the seat of which would be more than a thousand miles removed from some of them?"

To such an indignity freemen never would submit! Republican governments "are only calculated for a territory but small in its extent." The states must be the primary units of government on a scale as broad as the North American continent. An energetic national government would extinguish republican liberty, destroy the states, and quite possibly end in a "violent convulsion" out of which new governments, formed on principles unfavorable to liberty, would emerge.[26]

For all practical purposes, the states had been dissolved in Philadelphia. The preamble announced this compact to be between the people and the new central government; henceforth men would look to the federal city for protection, for succor, for guidance, for the ropes with which to bind their fellows.

The national government, Martin predicted, would grow fat and menacing on the taxes and duties it would impose upon the citizens of the States; it would "squeeze from them the little money they may acquire, the hard earnings of their industry, as you would squeeze the juice from an orange, till not a drop more can be extracted."[27] Tax collectors would harass the citizenry, invade their homes, and "sluice them at every vein as long as they have a drop of blood."[28] An overstatement, perhaps, at least for those who have never had a go-round with the IRS.*

---

* Patrick Henry warned that the federal tax-gatherer "may commit what oppression, make what distresses, he pleases, and ruin you with impunity; for how are you to tie his hands? Have you any sufficiently decided means of preventing him from sucking your blood by speculations, commissions, and fees?" (Elliot, *Debates*, Vol. III, 57). At least a local publican, who must live with those he mulcts, is vulnerable to a twinge of compassion. "I think a Continental collector will not be so likely to do us justice in collecting the taxes, as collectors of our own," said Nathaniel Barrell at the Massachusetts convention (ibid., Vol. II, 160). Even the tyrant, or his agents, may falter when their victims can look them in the eye.

The power to tax is the power to destroy, as a man never mistaken for an Anti-Federalist once said. Among those institutions destroyed would be the constituent units of the national government. The federal taxing power "is calculated to annihilate totally the state governments," said George Mason to the Virginia convention. State and national governments may tax concurrently, but in time "the one will destroy the other: the general government being paramount to, and in every respect more powerful than state governments, the latter must give way to the former."[29]

The states, said Martin, were "much better judges of the circumstances of their citizens, and what sum of money could be collected from them by direct taxation, and of the manner in which it could be raised, with the greatest ease and convenience to their citizens, than the general government could be."[30] Thus the taxing power ought to rest in the states—at least if the ease and convenience of the taxpayers are to be weighed, as they rarely are in the publican's scale.

In forbidding Maryland and her sisters from printing paper money, the drafters had also mislegislated. States had in the past "received great benefit from paper emissions."[31] Why should this option be forever foreclosed? Was all economic wisdom to be gathered within the fortified walls of the federal city? Likewise, Martin objected to the prohibition on states laying import and export duties without the consent of Congress. So long as such taxes were light, the revenue might fund the proper duties of the state. In any event, the call belonged—ought to belong—to the states themselves.

Martin also appealed to naked self-interest. Maryland lacked the extensive western territories of, say, Virginia. Soon enough these lands would be peopled, and so the gap between populous states and their smaller neighbors would widen. The sly Old Dominion had created the House of Representatives as the means of her continental dominion.

Maryland had delayed ratifying the Articles of Confederation in dissatisfaction over jurisdictional claims in the western lands. Martin was happy to rub raw that old wound.

Playing upon the meed mistrust Marylanders bore Virginia, Martin criticized Article IV, Section 3, which forbad the fissioning of states without the approval of the states concerned and Congress. Distended states were protected thereby, even though "every principle of justice and sound policy requires their dismemberment." Divide Virginia! Republics require smallness, compaction, affinity. Why should the ultramontane yeomanry have to bow to coastal elites to which they are bound not by affection or nativity but merely the exactions of the tax-gatherer? Such a condition would "justify even recourse to arms, to free themselves from, and to shake off, so ignominious a yoke." Maintaining overlarge states guaranteed civil war, and there was no question where Martin's sympathies would lie. No way should the doughty patriots of Maryland's militia march off to suppress the autonomous dreams of the people of Maine, of Franklin, of Vermont, of Kentucky.

Martin told the Maryland legislature, "By the principles of the American Revolution, arbitrary power *may* and *ought* to be resisted, even by arms if necessary. The time may come when it shall be the duty of a State, in order to preserve itself from the oppression of the general government, to have recourse to the sword."[32] The FBI would take a keen interest in such a statement today. Poor Luther would find himself on the No Fly List.

Separation was preferable to submission. Live free or die, as the license plate says. Or as Patrick Henry told the Virginia convention, "The first thing I have at heart is American liberty: the second thing is American union."[33] If the price of union is truckling to a centralized superstate, then to hell with union. New Englanders would entertain such thoughts in 1803 and 1814 and 1848; southerners would act on them in 1861. Martin, as if anticipating Jeff Davis and the Lost Cause, denied that states taking up arms against the union were committing treason. He called for such acts of rebellion to be "regulated by the laws of war and of nations."[34] Years later, the hotspurs of South Carolina and Georgia would wish that their nationalist forbears had listened to Luther Martin, as well as the Hartford Conventioneers of 1814.

Martin was not a man given to compromise, to splitting loaves, hairs, or infinitives. He exhorted the Old Line Staters to block that coup and reject the Constitution.

Yes, certain of the crudest Madisonian excrescences had been scraped off the finished product, but this Constitution was no ingenious blend of the federal and the national. The realm of the national government was seemingly without limit. Responsibility for promoting the general welfare was "coextensive with every possible object of human legislation," as Richard Henry Lee wrote.[35] Absent a Bill of Rights, where were the restraints upon this juggernaut?

The patriotic legend in which a hall full of dispassionate gods produced the most perfect instrument ever devised for republican self-rule had yet to congeal. Luther Martin wanted the Maryland legislature to know that behind the sealed and caulked doors mere men, not gods, bartered and schemed for advantage. If only they were gods, parleying in pantheon! But no, they dwelt on meaner things. A "great portion of that time," said Martin, "which ought to have been devoted calmly and impartially to consider what alterations in our federal government would be most likely to procure and preserve the happiness of the Union, was employed in a violent struggle on the one side to obtain all power and dominion in their own hands, and on the other to prevent it." The "aggrandizement of particular States and particular individuals, appears to have been much more the object sought after, than the welfare of our country."

The system under construction was injurious to Maryland, inimical to liberty, and incompatible with republican governance. Martin had opposed it, manfully and vocally, since the nationalist onslaught of early June. He had "endeavoured to act as became a free man, and the delegate of a free State." He had taken his stand against the most eminent men of his generation. He had no regrets.

He ended his address to the House of Delegates with a histrionic but heartfelt vow of poverty:

[S]o destructive do I consider the present system to the happiness of my country, I would cheerfully sacrifice that share of property with which Heaven has blessed a life of industry; I would reduce myself to indigence and poverty, and those who are dearer to me than my own existence I would intrust to the care and protection of that Providence, who hath so kindly protected myself, if on those terms only I could procure my country to reject those chains which are forged for it.[36]

If the damned thing were ratified, it would not be because Luther Martin was silent.

Martin's animadversions were met with derision and smears.

Oliver Ellsworth, a Connecticut delegate and snuff-addict pungently described by historian Robert Allen Rutland in *The Ordeal of the Constitution* (1966) as having a "facile pen and loose regard for the niceties of fact,"[37] stuck the shiv in his old Princeton classmate's back in an open letter of extraordinary truculence.

Ellsworth was one of those men (always to be with us) incapable of simple disagreement over a matter of principle or philosophy. He must impugn his interlocutor's motives, malign his character. He had not the courage to challenge directly the Anti-Federalists in Philadelphia, but in behavior typical of the polemical poltroon he aimed his poison darts at the Constitution's critics once he had put a safe distance between them and himself. Nor was he bound by strict regard for fact. Before lying about Martin, he had spread falsehoods about the Virginia Anti-Federalist Richard Henry Lee and compounded the lie by ascribing to Lee authorship of the essays of the "Federal Farmer," whom we now believe to be Melancton Smith of New York. (Smith was pointedly mocked for his anonymous essays by Alexander Hamilton in the New York convention.)

In a letter printed in the December 24, 1787, *Connecticut Courant* and quite devoid of seasonal charity, Ellsworth attacked Elbridge Gerry and George Mason for "treachery and falsehood." These men were not permitted to oppose the Constitution on federal (or anti-federal, as the term had been twisted) grounds. No, Mason was accused of "sore mortification" over the navigation clause and Gerry was upset that the convention had rejected his motion to redeem at nominal value worthless continental paper money, of which Ellsworth accused Gerry of possessing a hoard. The Bay Stater was said to be a squalid amalgam of "barefaced selfishness and injustice," animated by "the utmost rage and resentment."[38]

Gerry, nonplussed, responded to Ellsworth. He had made no such motion in the convention! (The notes of Madison et al., released decades too late to do any good, supported Gerry.) What on earth was Ellsworth (writing anonymously, of course) talking about?

Martin defended Gerry against this baseless charge in the January 18, 1788, *Maryland Journal*. His letter is sobriety reified. "I never heard Mr. Gerry or any other member introduce" such a proposal, he writes, accurately as it turns out. Moreover, "Mr. Gerry's opposition to the System was warm and decided," particularly in his fear that state militia were to be under the authority of the national government.[39]

Martin forbore from remarking upon his old Princeton classmate Ellsworth's atrocious manners and mendacity. He would pay for his tact.

Ellsworth (or so most historians believe; see note 40), writing as "The Landholder" (bondholder was more like it), savaged Martin in the Leap Day *Maryland Journal* of February 29, 1788.

"The day you took your seat," Landholder challenged Martin,

> must be long remembered by those who were present; nor will it be possible for you to forget the astonishment your behaviour almost instantaneously produced. You had scarcely time to read the propositions . . . when . . . you opened against them in a speech which held during two days, and which might have continued two months, but for those marks of fatigue and disgust you saw strongly expressed on whichever side of the house you turned your mortified eyes.

Landholder either misremembered or lied. Martin had taken his seat on June 9. His first motion, which Madison records in a short paragraph, came two days later. The next time he held the floor was on the 19th, when his remarks again occupy a brief paragraph in Madison. He had been sitting in convention for over two and a half weeks before his linguacious June 27–28 address.

Landholder indicted Martin for "endless garrulity" and "eternal volubility." He accused him of "memorable blunders." He misrepresented his arguments and twisted his views, though without a single available volume of the Madison-Yates-Lansing variorum the puzzled reader had no way to know this. The abuse went on and on: "[Y]ou exhausted the politeness of the Convention, which at length prepared to slumber when you rose to speak."[40]

That's good invective. These men, unlike our contemporary politicians, could write. Seldom did they resort to that indispensable factotum of the twentieth and twenty-first centuries, the ghostwriter. If we read Luther Martin or Oliver Ellsworth we may be sure, at least, that we are reading the unmediated thought of Luther Martin or Oliver Ellsworth and not Robert Sherwood or Ted Sorensen or Peggy Noonan. (Ellsworth was unfair to his old classmate, but still, one cannot help but spare a fond thought for a man who in his caducity recollected, "I have visited several countries, and I like my own the best. I have been in all the states of the Union, and Connecticut is the best state. Windsor is the pleasantest town in the state of Connecticut, and I have the pleasantest place in the town of Windsor. I am content, perfectly content, to die on the banks of the Connecticut.")[41]

Muck sticks. As Martin wrote years later, "There is a propensity in mankind to believe whatever tends to lessen the respectability of their fellow creatures."[42] Martin's reputation as the Man Who Wouldn't Shut Up is drawn primarily from Madison, William Pierce, and Landholder. So what if Landholder—secure in the knowledge that what happened in Independence Hall stayed in Independence Hall—upbraided Martin unfairly? His readers had no reason to doubt him, and posterity, to the extent that it cares any more about such antediluvian (perhaps anteimperium is the better word) matters, has swallowed the lie.

For the record, Clarkson and Jett count up the ballots for most voluble delegate:

> The most frequent speaker was Gouverneur Morris, who addressed that body on some 173 recorded occasions, this despite an initial handicap of not having arrived until July. Wilson of Pennsylvania spoke 168 times, Madison 161, Sherman 138, Mason 136, and, of particular interest, Ellsworth himself spoke 84 times. Further examination of the record shows that just over half of Martin's total of 53 "speeches" consisted of making or seconding a motion, as recorded in two or three lines each in Madison's and Yates's notes. On 16 occasions he made brief observations on the subject under discussion, the whole of which are reported in less than sixty lines in Farrand's *Records*. On not more than six occasions did he make any address which could conceivably be termed extended.[43]

Landholder minted the canard, Madison's snotty aside put it into wide circulation, and it would seem that no contrary evidence will ever be strong enough to remove it from the common currency. Luther Martin speaks fifty-three times and is the runamouth, Gouverneur Morris speaks 173 times and is the raconteur.

Martin's response to Ellsworth's attacks lacked the brevity, not to mention wit, of "I know you are but what am I?" In the first of his tripartite replies (*Maryland Journal*, March 3, 1788), he went on and on, as Luther was wont to do, establishing a personal convention chronology and saying nice things about Elbridge Gerry. In the second letter (*Maryland Journal*, March 18, 1788), he handily disposed of Ellsworth's strange charge of enmity between Martin and Gerry. (Landholder claimed that Gerry had delivered a devastating putdown of Martin after his speech on June 27—a sarcastic gem that Madison, Yates, and Lansing fail to record.) After his restrained performance in the first letter, Martin warms up his pillorying arm. He throws a brushback or two at Landholder, baron of "perversion and misrepresentation," creature with a "heart which would dishonour the midnight assassin," and creep "to whom falsehood appears more familiar than truth."

To Landholder's thrust that "You, alone, advocated the political heresy, that the people ought not to be trusted with the election of representatives," Martin's parry was a model of true federalist . . . not quite concision, but perception:

> In a state government, I consider all power flowing immediately from the people in their individual capacity, and that the people, in their individual capacity, have, and ought to have the right of choosing delegates in a state legislature, the business of which is to make laws, regulating their concerns, as individuals, and operating upon them as such; but in a federal government, formed over free states, the power flows from the people, and the right of choosing delegates belongs to them only mediately through their respective state governments which are the members composing the federal government, and from whom all its power immediately proceeds; to which state governments, the choice of the federal delegates immediately belongs.[44]

Surely that passage has a clarity that is often missing in *The Federalist Papers*. He also flashes wit, which Publius assiduously avoids. Landholder, Martin gibes, may not be an arrant liar; "perhaps, as the Convention was prepared to slumber whenever I rose, the Landholder, among others, might have sunk into sleep, and at that very moment might have been feasting his imagination with the completion of his ambitious views, and dreams of future greatness."

Landholder's poison arrows had hit their target. Envenomed, Martin returns again and again to his imputed tedium. He imagines his auditors in Philadelphia—"one gaping here, another yawning there, a third slumbering in this place, and a fourth snoring in that"—so united in their contempt for him that it might have "put to flight all my original arrogance" and led him to "become convinced of my comparative nothingness."[45]

Buried in the verbiage of Martin's multiple replies is a passage of a certain predictive power.

> [I]f my rising to speak had such a somnific influence on the Convention . . . I have no doubt the time will come, should this system be adopted, when my countrymen will ardently wish I had never left the Convention, but remained there to the last, daily administering to my associates the salutary opiate. Happy, thrice happy, would it have been for my country, if the whole of that time had been devoted to sleep, or been a blank in our lives, rather than employed in forging its chains.[46]

Chains? The Constitution? Were there really men who saw in those magnificent sentences the shackles and fetters of tyranny? Well, yes. Patrick Henry, for one, who plaintively asked the Virginia ratifying convention: "Whither is the spirit of America gone? Whither is the genius of America fled? . . . When the American spirit was in its youth, the language of America was different: liberty, sir, was then the primary object. . . . But now, Sir, the American spirit, assisted by the ropes and chains of consolidation, is about to convert this country into a powerful and mighty empire."[47]

Or as a Charleston poet lamented:

In five short years of Freedom weary grown
We quit our plain republics for a throne[48]

How to keep the chains off? Reject the Constitution, thundered Luther Martin. Failing that, cut the king-like president down to a republican size. No veto for the executive. Restrict his pardoning power. Make him ineligible for a second term. Let the Senate nominate federal judges. Deny the national government the ability to suspend habeas corpus. Insist upon a bill of rights. Protect trial by jury ("the surest barrier against arbitrary power"),[49] freedom of speech, liberty of the press. Prohibit the import of slaves.

Oops. This last is one of those inconvenient facts which fall through the cracks. While Benjamin Franklin is lauded as the antislavery conscience of Philadelphia, it was Luther Martin who proposed that the Constitution ban the import of slaves immediately, not a score of years hence.

Martin warned that the continuance of slavery "ought to be considered as justly exposing us to the displeasure and vengeance of Him who is equally Lord of all, and Who views with equal eye the poor African slave and his American master." We had achieved our independence from Great Britain by our petitions and supplications to that God who had endowed all his creatures, great and small, with liberties that the declarers of American independence had called self-evident. What rank hypocrisy—what sacrilege—what "solemn mockery of, and insult to" God—it was to not only offer the capacious shelter of the Constitution for this cruel institution but to actually encourage it through the three-fifths rule.

Slavery, "the only branch of commerce which is *unjustifiable in its nature*," was countenanced, even promoted, by the Philadelphia document. In other areas, the drafters had not scrupled to strengthen beyond reasonable bounds the prepotency of the central state—why, it was even to determine weights and measures and bar Maryland from emitting paper money—yet they had interdicted the one ability the national government ought to possess: that of banning immediately the import of slaves, and of providing for the "gradual abolition" of manowning.[50]

Martin ridiculed the three-fifths clause. What an "absurdity" it was, "increasing the power of a State in making laws for freemen in proportion as that State violated the rights of freedom."[51] If the Founders were sincere in uttering those pretty hymns to freedom, then why not count slaves in apportioning taxes but discount them in determining representation? Create incentives for liberty.

He contemned the circumlocutory constitutional phrase "such persons," which was a roundabout way of saying "slaves." The Framers "anxiously sought to avoid the admission of expressions which might be odious in the ears of Americans," sneered Martin, "although they were willing to admit into their system those things which the expressions signified."[52] (How unfair that a man capable of such acuity should be remembered, thanks to Madison, for incoherence.)

The identification of Anti-Federalism with antislavery (and, conversely, the Constitution with slavery) is one of those historical embarrassments from which Madisonian courtiers avert their eyes before quickly changing the subject. The Maryland Antis were not alone in standing against the traffic in men. Melancton Smith in New York damned the document for protecting "those people who were so wicked as to keep slaves."[53] George Mason, at the Virginia convention, called the trade "diabolical"; any document that could permit its continuation for twenty years was so horrid that "I cannot express my detestation of it." Casting his eyes down at Georgia and South Carolina, he declared, "I would not admit the Southern States into the Union unless they agree to the discontinuance of this disgraceful trade."

Madison, in response, defended the twenty-year allowance as the price of union. And besides, he added, whereas under the Articles there was no guarantee that a sister state would return a runaway slave, the solons of Philadelphia had decreed that "no person held to service or labor in one state, under the laws thereof, escaping into another, shall, in consequence of any law or regulation therein, be discharged from such service or labor; but shall be delivered up on claim of the party to whom such service or labor shall be due."[54] States' rights smiled on the runaway slave; a consolidated general government would remand Eliza and Little Eva to their rightful owners.[†]

Martin and Samuel Chase, the twin pillars of Maryland Anti-Federalism, were to be Honorary-Counselors of the "Maryland Society for promoting the Abolition of Slavery, and the Relief of Free Negroes and others unlawfully held in Bondage," established on September 8, 1789. The society's constitution—unlike the U.S. Constitution against which Martin and Chase had contended so strenuously and vainly—declared that

> The common Father of mankind created all men free and equal; and his great command is, that we love our neighbor as our-

---

[†] Of course, divisions on moral issues are seldom neat and clean. Patrick Henry warned the Virginia convention that in authorizing the general government to provide for the common defense, the Constitution foreshadowed abolition. Not that Henry had any particular love of the peculiar institution, but as Mr. Give-Me-Liberty-or-Give-Me-Death said, "As much as I deplore slavery, I see that prudence forbids its abolition" (Elliot, *Debates*, Vol. II, 227). Dear prudence.

selves—doing unto all men as we would they should do unto us. The human race, however varied in color or intellects, are all justly entitled to liberty; and it is the duty and the interest of nations and individuals, enjoying every blessing of freedom, to remove this dishonor of the Christian character from amongst them.[55]

Now, it is true that as of 1790 Martin owned six slaves, but hey, who among us does not traffic in little hypocrisies? (While the society's constitution barred slaveowners from membership, it did allow for their appointment as Honorary-Counselors, thus Martin's title.)

The society was more than a mere public assertion of virtue. It helped slaves sue for their freedom, it passed abolitionist petitions, and it spread the word for manumission. In his practice, Martin represented Negroes asserting their claim to freedom—but he also appeared as counsel for slavemasters seeking to reclaim their human property. The law may be a jealous mistress, but she permits her paramours to work both sides of the street.

Like the other Anti-Federalists, Martin demanded a Bill of Rights, though he noted that "had the government been formed upon principles truly federal, as I wished it, legislating over and acting upon the states only in their collective or political capacity, and not on individuals, there would have been no need of a bill of rights. . . ." It was the overreach of the Constitution, which presumed to legislate upon states and individuals, that necessitated a Bill of Rights.

But then nullifying the states was the intent of the Framers. "I most sacredly believe," Martin wrote to Landholder in a letter published in the *Maryland Journal* of March 21, 1788, that "their object is the total abolition and destruction of all state governments, and the erection on their ruins of one great and extensive empire, calculated to aggrandize and elevate its rulers and chief officers far above the common herd of mankind, to enrich them with wealth, and to encircle them with honours and glory. . . ."[56] You can scoff at this flight of fancy, or you can consider the careers of Lyndon Baines Johnson and Richard V. Cheney.

Martin foresaw a national state that, equipped for aggressive war, would wage aggressive war. Thus, Martin and Elbridge Gerry proposed to limit the size of the peacetime standing army, that "engine of arbitrary power, which has so often and so successfully been used for the subversion of freedom." No such luck. Posterity would have to rely on the "will and pleasure" of future Congresses to idle that engine.[57]

As the New Jersey legislature informed the Congress in 1778, "A standing army, a military establishment, and every appendage thereof, in time of peace, is totally abhorrent from the ideas and principles of this State."[58] No rhetorical damnation could fully compass this evil. "[H]ad I an arm like Jove," swore Major Samuel Nason in the Massachusetts convention, "I would hurl from the globe those villains that would dare attempt to establish in our country a standing army."[59] Only a supine people, fit for subjection, would consent to such a humiliation.

The militia was the palladium of freedom. Martin proposed, unsuccessfully, to bar the central government from calling up a state militia for duty out of state. Our neighbors in the National Guard, cruelly separated from their families and the places they call home, might wish he had succeeded.

Sketching a worst-case scenario, Martin asked the legislators of his state to imagine the Congress ordering the whole militia of Maryland to the remotest part of the Union, and keep[ing] them in service as long as they think proper, without being in any respect dependent upon the Government of Maryland for this unlimited exercise of power over its citizens— All of whom, from the lowest to the greatest, may, during such service, be subjected to military law, and tied up and whipped at the halbert, like the meanest of slaves.[60]

When Martin said "remote," he had Georgia on his mind. As for Honduras, Berlin, and Iraq—not in his most horrific delirium tremens hallucinations could he have imagined militia dispatched thereto.

Martin and the Wilson-Hamilton-Madison axis entertained diametrically opposed conceptions of the militia. To the latter, it was an offensive force, tethered not to its native ground, capable of traveling great distances in order to squelch revolts, stifle particularistic eruptions, and ensure obedience to the central authority. To Luther Martin and the Anti-Federalists, the militia was a bulwark of home liberty. It was defensive in nature. An organic entity, rooted within self-governing communities, it protected the people of the state against the depredations of potential invaders—including the standing army of the general government. If Maryland should cede control of her militia to the federal authority, how could she defend herself should the president-king order his myrmidons to "oppress and enslave" the freemen of Maryland?[61] Do not relinquish the militia, Martin begged his neighbors; do not enter this union defenseless against the treacheries of designing men. He failed, of course. Surely no American president would treat the militia as a legion of slaves, to be marched off to faraway places to fight wars for profit and conquest.

The national government, he cautioned, would someday call up militia members "from any particular state without its permission" and send them upon "remote and improper services"[62]—and to judge Martin's predictive powers you may consult the case of *Perpich v. Defense* (1990), in which the U.S. Supreme Court brushed aside the objections of Minnesota's state government to the ordering of the Minnesota National Guard, heir to the state militia of the Founding era, to Central America. The Empire, ruled the Court, can send state guard units wherever in hell it wishes to, no matter how loudly the governor and legislature of the affected state might complain.

Luther Martin, like the vast majority of Anti-Federalists *and* Federalists, did not imagine a United States that sent ships and soldiers across the great oceans to write constitutions for other nations:

> I feel no Quixotic desire of proselyting the world to the republic system; no hatred or contempt for those who live under governments of a different form; nor do I think the man, who believes a republican government the best adapted for all nations, without regard to their habits and manners, and who would wish to compel its adoption in all climes and in all countries, a whit more wise or less cruel, than the tyrant, who took into his head the barbarous whim, by stretching or lopping every individual who came in his way, to reduce them all to the standard of the same bedstead. The man who pretends to expect, by universally republicanising the world, to effect the perfectability of human nature, the perfectability of human reason, and the perfectability of human happiness, or to introduce a millennium on the earth, will ever by me be considered an enthusiastic visionary . . . or a crafty villainous imposter.[63]

By failing to rein in the standing army, the Framers had left the door open to crafty and villainous militaristic proselytizers. But the Constitution was inadequate in so many other ways as well.

Term limits, a basic feature of the Articles, were gone. "Nothing is so essential to the preservation of a republican government as a periodical rotation," insisted George Mason.[64] Even many friends of the Constitution regretted their absence. G. Livingston of the soi-disant aristocratic Livingstons of New York envisioned a federal city surrounded by "an impenetrable wall of adamant and gold, the wealth of the whole country flowing into it." Behind the wall dwelled a cosseted set of lotus-eating senatorial lifers:

> In this Eden they will reside with their families, distant from the observation of the people. In such a situation, men are apt to forget their dependence, lose their sympathy, and contract selfish habits. . . . The senators will associate only with men of their own class, and thus become strangers to the condition of the common people. They should not only return, and be obliged to live with the people, but return to their former rank of citizenship, both to revive their sense of dependence, and to gain a knowledge of the country.[65]

Martin foresaw what would happen to well-meaning provincials who went to Washington afire with idealism. "If he has a family," Martin said of a typical senator, "he will take his family with him to the place where the government shall be fixed; that will become his home, and there is every reason to expect, that his future views and prospects will centre in the favors and emoluments of the general government. . . . [H]e is *lost* to his *own State*."[66]‡

---

‡ Thus reads the epitaph on the 1995–2007 Republican majority in the House of Representatives. If your congressman is anything like the whore who represents

A national Congress, said the Anti-Federalists, must be un-wieldy or tyrannical. As Yates and Lansing explained to Governor Clinton, "if the general legislature was composed of so numerous a body of men as to represent the interests of all the inhabitants of the United States . . . the expense of supporting it would become intolerably burdensome," while "if a few only were vested with a power of legislation, the interests of a great majority of the inhabit-ants of the United States must necessarily be unknown."[67]

Thomas Paine, in *Common Sense* (1776), proposed that each colony send "at least thirty" representatives to a Congress of "at least 390" members.[68] George Mason rang the same chime in the Virginia convention. The legislature of the Old Dominion was far more sensitive to and knowledgeable of local conditions than would be Virginia's congressional delegation, he stated. For how do Virginia's legislators obtain their information? "They get it from one hundred and sixty representatives dispersed through all parts of the country." Virginia's members of the U.S. House of Repre-sentatives, by contrast, would be "but ten—chosen, if not wholly, yet mostly, from the higher order of the people—from the great, the wealthy—the *well-born* . . . that aristocratic idol—that flatter-ing idea—that *exotic* plant."[69] Enervated, mincing, ennui-ridden dainties to whom the yeomanry were a herd, a mass, a distasteful bolus good only for taxing and sending off to fight.

Congressional districts were far too large; Congress was oli-garchically small. As the Anti-Federalist writer "Philadelphiensis"

---

my district, upon his defeat he did not pack up the wife and kids and mistress and assorted pages and head back home to edit the local paper or sell insurance from his office at the corner of Elm and Oak Streets. No, he extended the lease on his condo in hideous Occupied Virginia and started cashing in on his public service as a lobbyist, a consultant, a leech on the corpse of the Republic.

warned, "65 representatives, and . . . 26 senators, with a king at their head, are to possess powers, that extend to the *lives*, the *liberties*, and *property* of every citizen in America."[70] Ninety-one members constituted the whole of Congress, forty-six made a quorum, so just two dozen men could enact laws binding upon every living creature from the White Mountains of New Hampshire to the Okefenokee Swamp of Georgia. "Can the liberties of three millions of people be securely trusted in the hands of twenty-four men?"[71] asked Melancton Smith. The question was the answer.

To be fair, Madison had moved on July 10 to double the size of the House of Representatives to 130. The additional expense would be minimal, he said. Sounding like an Anti-Federalist—or like the Madison of ten years after this space in time—he opined that a House of only 65 members "would be too sparsely taken from the people, to bring with them all the local information which would be frequently wanted."[72] His motion carried only Virginia and Delaware. Madison was referring to a Congress in which each member represented about 30,000 persons; today, the average congressional district contains 650,000 persons.

To call the Anti-Federalists proponents of "states' rights" is to miss the point. Or rather it is to minimize the point. They were decentralists who guarded the rights of the states against usurpation by the federal government. But the vast majority of them would not object to—indeed, they would have encouraged—the transfer of state powers to even more local jurisdictions. Samuel Spencer, in the North Carolina convention, went so far as to suggest the further division of the states: "If the United States were to consist of ten times as many states, they might all have a degree of harmony. Nothing would be wanting but some cement for their connection."[73]

Though consensus historians have stressed the dialectic of 1787–88, in which Anti-Federalist concerns are incorporated by the Federalists into the Bill of Rights and the good vibrations echo through the land, in fact the debate featured a conflict of almost irreconcilable visions. They were as antipodal as the concepts of big and small.

Lecturing the Pennsylvania ratifying convention, James Wilson expressed the megalomaniacal universalism of the consolidators: "Numerous states yet unformed, myriads of the human race, who will inhabit regions hitherto uncultivated, were to be affected by the result of their proceedings. It was necessary, therefore, to form their calculations on a scale commensurate to a large portion of the globe."

The problem with such a scale is that its incremental measurements are too large to weigh Weare, New Hampshire, Poughkeepsie, New York, or Hillsborough, North Carolina. Wilson was "lost in astonishment at the vastness of the prospect before us,"[74] and in his awestruckness he lost sight of the individuated persons and townships and avenues that make up that prospect. He saw a forest without trees. Men with such purblindness, alas, are given to clearcutting those trees.

The "freedom and happiness of the citizen," said Luther Martin, can be preserved only when the territory ruled by a government is "*small* in its extent"[75]—say, the size of Maryland.

Republics could not thrive but in small territories. In large polities, with a multitude of interests and welter of circumstances, citizens would be ruled "by those who have neither knowledge of our situation, nor a common interest with us, nor a fellow-feeling for us," said George Mason.[76] Manhattan cosmopolites would write laws governing rural Utah Mormons, and unplaced

Floridians would draft diktats applying to Burlington hippies. Hamilton asserted that "the people of a large country may be represented as truly as those of a small one,"[77] but evidence for this claim is hard to find—like pickpockets in a mob.

Against the Anti-Federalist conviction that a republic was suitable only for a small area in which citizens could know and be known to one another, James Madison asserted the superiority of sprawl. In *Federalist* 10, he argued on behalf of a "large over a small republic" because the former would have "representatives whose enlightened views and virtuous sentiments render them superior to local prejudices and to schemes of injustice." (The staggering inaccuracy of this prophecy has not in the least detracted from the éclat accorded this essay by students of American government.) A state whose jurisdiction extends over vast territories is unlikely to fall for any such "improper or wicked project" as paper money or "an equal division of property," writes Madison.[78] Local governments he views as idiosyncratic and unpredictable; a national state would stifle eccentricities under a blanket of bland uniformity.

The local is denigrated throughout *The Federalist Papers*. The "great interests of the nation," writes Madison in *Federalist* 46, "have suffered on a hundred [occasions] from an undue attention to the local prejudices, interests, and views of the particular States."[79] To which the Anti-Federalist might reply that Madison misses the point. The "great interests of the nation" are nothing more than the sum of local interests. The United States thrive only if Maryland and Albany and the Berkshires, in their own particularized and unduplicable ways, thrive first.

Hamilton, of course, was even more hostile to that which impeded the national; were it within his power he would have abolished the states entirely. Rebutting Melancton Smith in the New York convention, Hamilton discoursed on the glory of "large districts of election," where men are not known to each other and "factions and cabals are little known."[80] This is classic wish-is-father-to-the-thought-fulness, but natheless it is the Hamiltonian bunk that has passed down to us as the holy writ of the Federalist genii of 1787. We do not notice—because Hamilton did not deign to answer, except to light a strawman ablaze—convention president George Clinton's response to the West Indian adulterer:

> In the state, the legislators, being generally known, and under the perpetual observation of their fellow-citizens, feel strongly the check resulting from the facility of communication and discovery. In a small territory, maladministration is easily corrected, and designs unfavorable to liberty frustrated and punished. But in large confederacies, the alarm excited by small and gradual encroachments rarely extends to the distant members, or inspires a general spirit of resistance.[81]

Hamilton suavely replied that Clinton's reasoning, which is "generally discarded by wise and discerning men,"[82] would lead, ineluctably, to dissolution, and ought not to be taken seriously.

Besides, Hamilton purred, disingenuously, the state governments, secure in the loyalty of the people, will "make encroachments on the national authority," not the other way around.[83]

The Antis gasped in disbelief. Which government, the national or the state, could raise armies? they asked. Which had an apparently unlimited power of taxation? There was no comparison; the federal city would, in time, reduce the states to nullities "who shall meet once in a year to make laws for regulating the height of your fences and the repairing of your roads."[84]

The iron curtain of silence draped over Independence Hall in May 1787 and still intact in 1788 enabled Hamilton to misrepresent—no, let us speak frankly; he was never much good at the code duello anyway so I ain't afeard—it enabled Hamilton to *lie* at the New York convention about what had gone on in Philadelphia. He came off in Poughkeepsie as a nationalist who was also a solicitous friend to state governments. When John Lansing exposed his dissimulation, Hamilton, confident that the truth lay buried underneath so many vows of silence, acted the affronted statesman. The resultant "warm personal altercation between those gentlemen," as the official report of the New York convention characterized the row, lasted two days.[85] Hamilton was long dead before the extent of his lying was known. And by that time, the Founders had been cast in marble; the aspersions of a nonentity like Lansing were so many pigeon droppings on the statuary.

The very laxity of a confederation is much of its strength; for happy are those who govern themselves, and how miserable is the provincial at the mercy of remote rulers. Anti-Federalists were fond of the Swiss example, in which autonomous cantons confederated for mutual defense. Solemn men of substance scoffed that the confederation under the Articles was a rope of sand, but what metonymical rope of government, one wonders, would they wish to be bound by?

Herbert Storing, editor of *The Complete Anti-Federalist*, took note of "the conservative posture of the opposition."[86] Martin, sounding rather like Russell Kirk, deprecated the Federalists' "proneness for novelty and change."[87] The Articles, embodiment of the Revolution of 1776, had barely been tried and not necessarily found wanting.

John Tyler, father of the tenth president, told the Virginia convention that the Constitution "contains a variety of powers too dangerous to be vested in any set of men whatsoever. Its power of direct taxation, the supremacy of the laws of the Union [thanks, Luther!], and of treaties, are exceedingly dangerous."[88] The liberties for which the patriots of 1776 had fought were being forfeited, thrown away not in some dire emergency—for where was the crisis impelling this counterrevolution?—but at the behest of the notional James Madison and lackeys of the moneyed interest such as Alexander Hamilton.

"In this Constitution, sir, we have departed widely from the principles and political faith of '76, when the spirit of liberty ran high, and danger put a curb on ambition," said Thomas Tredwell, a Plattsburgh, New York, attorney and Princetonian (class of 1764) who delivered one of the finest and least remembered speeches in any of the ratifying conventions. "Here we find no security for the rights of individuals, no security for the existence of our state governments; here is no bill of rights, no proper restriction of power; our lives, our property, and our consciences, are left wholly at the mercy of the legislature, and the powers of the judiciary may be extended to any degree short of almighty."

Tredwell was the poet of the Anti-Federalists, and if his imagery shaded into purple, well, when "the dagger of Ambition is now pointed at the fair bosom of Liberty," who can bother with minimalism? Tredwell deserves remembrance if only for his description of the federal city to come: a place "where men are to live, without labor, upon the fruit of the labors of others; this political hive, where all the drones in society are to be collected to feed on the honey of the land."[89] K Street, thou art Tredwell Alley.

The federal judiciary would run roughshod over the states, usurping, poaching, interfering with matters properly reserved to the states and arrogating unto itself an imperial portfolio. The federal courts, said George Mason, were unlimited in their jurisdiction; "their effect and operation will be utterly to destroy the state governments; for they will be the judges how far their laws will operate." In time, "every object of private property" will be swept into the bailiwick of the expansive federal court system.[90] No matter would be too trifling to "make a federal case out of."

The Federalists denied this. Richard Dobbs Spaight, who seldom spoke in Philadelphia, assured the ratifying convention in North Carolina that the jurisdictions of federal and state courts were "separate and distinct" and never the twain shall meet.[91] The realm of the former was strictly delimited. Trust us on this, said the Federalists, with a wink to posterity and Earl Warren.

Again and again, throughout the debates in the states, Anti-Federalists predict the engorgement of the central government and the debilitation of the states. The Federalists, unable to hang their denial on any constitutional peg, resort to airy reassurances. Agents of the federal government, they say, are concurrently citizens of the states. Why should they wish to disable the states, to dispossess their neighbors of their rights? Weak government, assert the Federalists, is the immediate threat; the menacing enhancement of this paper-drawn federal system is a remote threat, hardly to be feared. Besides, all parties tacitly agree that the first president will be George Washington, a man whom even the most suspicious Anti-Federalist would trust with his liberties. How much more protective of our liberties would the Framers have been, one wonders, if the putative first president was a man less universally respected than Washington: say, John Hancock? (Consider South Carolina delegate Pierce Butler's admission in a letter of May 1788 that the president's "Powers are full great, and greater than I was disposed to make them. Nor . . . do I believe they would have been so great had not many of the members cast their eyes towards General Washington as President; and shaped their Ideas of the Powers to be given to a President, by their opinions of his Virtue. So that the Man, who by his Patriotism and Virtue, Contributed largely to the Emancipation of his Country, may be the Innocent means of its being, when He is lay'd low, oppress'd."[92] The Federalists, so often credited with farsightedness, saw no farther than the noble Washington. Only Martin, Lansing, Yates, and the dissentients could envision Lyndon B. Johnson or George W. Bush.)

The Federalists, claimed the Antis, were top-heavy with lawyers, aristocrats, and speculators. Of the Massachusetts convention Robert Rutland has written, "Conspicuously absent from the Antifederalist benches were college graduates, lawyers, merchants, or men who felt more comfortable on a countinghouse highboy than on a milk stool."[93] Farmers and useful mechanicks and placed men (*not* placemen) dominated the Anti-Federalist ranks, and how were men of such modest means to be elected to the U.S. Congress?

Melancton Smith said of Congress that "the style in which the members live will probably be high; circumstances of this kind will render the place of a representative not a desirable one to sensible, substantial men, who have been used to walk in the plain and frugal paths of life." Only men of wealth, of conspicuous achievement, of fame, will win election to the national legislature. "A substantial yeoman, of sense and discernment, will hardly ever be chosen" for this most unrepresentative crop of representatives.[94]

Smith, Tredwell, Martin, and the Antis were the unlionized. The press was agin' 'em: perhaps a dozen newspapers in all the country, or about one in ten, can be identified as Anti-Federalist.

Yet Martin was not without defenders. "Philadelphiensis," the young University of Pennsylvania tutor Benjamin Workman, championed in the *Independent Gazeteer* "that honest man and firm patriot, MR. MARTIN." Cecelia M. Kenyon describes "Philadelphiensis" as "flamboyant," as though he were the Harvey Fierstein of the Anti-Federalists, but he was more fiery than Fierstein. Witness "Philadelphiensis" in action:

> Is that man an *incendiary* who advocates the unalienable rights of the people? Is he an enemy to America who endeavors to protect the *oppressed* from the *oppressor*; who opposes a conspiracy against the liberties of his country, concerted by a few *tyrants*, whose views are to lord it over the rest of their fellow citizens, to trample the poorer part of the people under their feet, that they may be rendered their servants and slaves? If such a writer is an incendiary, and an enemy to America, then I glory in the character. A conspiracy against the freedom of America, both deep and dangerous, has been formed by an infernal junto of demagogues. Our thirteen free commonwealths are to be consolidated into one *despotic monarchy*.[95]

Martin concurred. The men with whom he had disputed in Philadelphia were as much monsters as gods. "[A]mbition and interest had so far blinded the understanding of some of the principal framers of the Constitution," he wrote in the *Maryland Journal*, "that while they were labouring to erect a fabrick by which they themselves might be exalted and benefited, they were rendered insensible to the sacrifice of the freedom and happiness of the states and their citizens, which must, inevitably be the conseqence."[96]

His campaign against ratification was fought in newspapers and taverns, and while he was at home in both venues, his tendency to maunder and harangue may have been in better check in the former.

He fought unto the last ditch, then he fell silent. In a grim irony, Luther Martin was unable to address the Maryland ratifying convention of April 1788. He was beset by laryngitis, the common cold of the loquacious, which, as a sardonic observer noted, "saved a great deal of time & money to the state."[97]

Six states had already ratified the Constitution when seventy-four delegates (two others never showed) met in springtime Annapolis. The votes in the Delaware, New Jersey, and Georgia conventions had been unanimous; only Massachusetts (187–168) had been close. But New Hampshire, North Carolina, and Rhode Island all appeared headed for the Anti-Federal column, and the outcomes in New York and Virginia were uncertain. From the Old Dominion, James Madison looked nervously to Maryland, writing George Washington on April 10 that "The difference between even a postponement and adoption in Maryland, may in the nice balance of parties here, possibly give a fatal advantage to that which opposes the Constitution."[98] If Maryland were to delay, even till June, then Virginia might reject the document and all the pretty plans of the consolidators would be strewn in pieces across the ground.

The Maryland ratification forces had let no Martin broadside go unanswered. "[W]e common people," replied "Sidney" in the February 29, 1788, *Maryland Journal*, "are more properly citizens of America, than any particular state."[99] Words to warm the chill hearts of James Wilson and Alexander Hamilton! Just how much the Federalists cherished the "common people" was revealed when the state senate resolved to set a minimum property qualification of five hundred pounds for delegates to the ratifying convention, a condition struck out by the Anti-Federalists in the House of Delegates.

The Antis were scant in Annapolis. In early April the counties of Anne Arundel, Harford, and Baltimore each elected four Anti-Federalists, but this distinguished dozen was far outnumbered. (Only six thousand of the twenty-five thousand eligible voters in the state had bothered to vote for delegates.) Martin, now a resident of Baltimore, was elected to represent Harford County, in which he did not live. This was an offense against the integrity of place, but the Federalists, with their overwhelming majority, didn't bother to rule Martin ineligible.

Although the convention was gaveled to order on Monday, April 21, Anti-Federalist leaders Martin, Samuel Chase, and William Paca did not show up until Thursday—a delay that permitted the Federalists to approve a streamlined set of rules barring consideration of "any particular part" of the proposed federal government.[100] Only an up or down vote on the whole package would be permitted.

The Antis quite sincerely desired a bill of rights as a rampart of liberty. But a happy consequence of ratifying with amendments would be a second national convention to collate the proposed amendments and perhaps more narrowly define the broad grants of power within the Constitution.

On Friday, April 25, William Paca, a lawyer who in best striving American fashion had married into the riches of the slave-supported Wye Hall plantation, rose to offer several amendments restricting the national authority. The majority forbade him even to read his proposals, let alone have them debated by the convention. For two days the Antis protested: "The advocates of the government, although repeatedly called on, and earnestly requested, to answer the objections, if not just, remained inflexibly silent." Having gagged the opposition and swallowed their own tongues, the Constitution men ratified by a vote of 63–11. The renegade Anti-Federalist was Paca, who explained that he had so voted in "full confidence" that the defects in the charter would be remedied by useful amendments.[101] These he offered once again; this time the majority indulged him, appointing a committee of thirteen (which did not include Mr. Martin) to vet the proposed addenda.

The committee recommended thirteen of these. They provided for, among other things, jury trial, freedom of the press, protection against search and seizure, and acknowledgment that "Congress shall exercise no power but what is expressly delegated by the Constitution."[102]

The amendments rejected by the committee reveal the deeper fears harbored by Anti-Federalists. One would have outlawed a standing army in peacetime unless authorized by two-thirds majorities in each house of Congress. Another barred the militia from marching "beyond the limits of an adjoining state" without the consent of the state government. Others protected "religious liberty," the right to petition, and state constitutions against the encroachment of treaties.[103]

In any event, the Federalists, after this brief display of lenity, perhaps realized that a huge majority need give no quarter to the minority. A motion to adjourn without delay or taking action on the committee's recommendations passed on the following Monday, 47–27. The twelve Anti-Federalists, Martin and the betrayed Paca among them, issued a minority report stating: "We consider the proposed form of national government as very defective, and that the liberty and happiness of the people will be endangered if the system be not greatly changed and altered."[104]

Historian Philip A. Crowl described Maryland's Anti-Federalists as an amalgam of "[p]arochialism, economic and political radicalism, libertarianism, and self-interest."[105] One might emend this to read "localism, equalitarianism, the liberty-minded, and those committed to small-scale democratic self-rule," but that would be coloring outside the lines.

Among the band of Anti-Federalists was William Pinkney, who would later serve as attorney general of Maryland and the United States (under James Madison). Pinkney was "a perfect contrast to Martin," according to Roger B. Taney. A corset-cinched dandy who appeared at court with his hands wrapped in ballroom-quality gloves, he spoke with a kind of ornate precision that struck his auditors as daintily Federalist. Taney, comparing these mismatched bookends of the Maryland bar, said, "I have seen [Pinkney] writhe as if in pain when he was listening to Martin speaking in his slovenly way, in broken sentences, using the most indefensible vulgarisms, and sometimes mispronouncing his words."[106]

Pinkney had no need of wincing in Annapolis. Martin was muted. George Washington, hearing of the results, wrote Madison on May 2, 1788:

"Mr. Chace [sic], it is said, made a display of all his eloquence. Mr. Mercer discharged his whole Artillery of inflammable matter—and Mr. Martin did something—I know not what—but presume with vehemence—yet no converts were made—no, not one."[107]

Maryland had ratified, overwhelmingly. Martin fought no more forever. He reconciled himself to the Constitution, even came to appreciate its masterly design. My favorite actor of recent years, Warren Oates, used to call himself a "constitutional anarchist." Maybe that's what Luther Martin was.

Martin, like the Massachusetts non-signer Elbridge Gerry, "could not see beyond his nose," sniffed Catherine Drinker Bowen,[108] but then myopia has its often uncredited virtues. It encourages a sense of political modesty, a keen awareness of the limits of one's knowledge, a decent respect for one's neighbors.

And really, just how myopic was Martin's vision? Was he not lynx-eyed in seeing the centripetal course upon which the Constitution set the government of the United States? Robert Rutland, for one, argues that the Anti-Federalists took the longer view: "The immediate future was not worrisome, but they fretted about 'unborn generations.' They feared that under the Constitution Americans would owe their allegiance to some distant Colossus where the emphasis would be on ceremonies and forms rather than a better life for the people."[109]

The Anti-Federalists typically are accused of failing to rise above parochialism, or to "raise their eyes above the rooftops" of their villages,[110] and what a queer indictment that is: they respected gravity and they focused their vision on subjects within their purview. Yet it is the untethered and unfocused who win history's plaudits!

The margins in the state conventions bespeak the hotly contested nature of the question. In Massachusetts, the nationalizers won by a vote of 187–168. New Hampshire's convention ratified by 57–47. The vote in Virginia was 89–79; that in New York was 30–27. North Carolina, with its "politics of resistance to distant power and protection of local liberties," in Michael Lienesch's phrase,[111] at first rejected the Constitution before ratifying it on November 21, 1789, almost two years after Delaware had become the first state to endorse the charter. Finally, Rhode Island, or "Rogue Island," as she was known, officially joined the Union on May 29, 1790, by a vote of 34–32. She had resisted for as long as she could, even under such threats as that of Boston Judge Francis Dana, who called for "a bold politician" to "seize upon the occasion their abominable antifederal conduct presents, for annihilating them as a separate member of the union" and divvying up the state between Massachusetts and Connecticut.[112]

The Federalists won the debate of 1787–88, and the defenders of the Articles, the libertarians, the decentralists, the paper-money populists, the backcountry philosophers, were off to historical Coventry. In time, it was as though they had never existed; they were subsumed under the consensus model of American historiography that snuffs and then quietly buries our dissenters. Defenders of limited and decentralized governance would even call themselves "constitutionalists," though it was the opponents of the Constitution who were their real ancestors. Sam Adams became a beer, Elbridge Gerry a rigged election district, George Mason a university with a free-market economics department and an underdog basketball team, Patrick Henry a college for homeschoolers, and Luther Martin . . . nothing.

The counterrevolution of 1787 enshrined the consolidators in the American pantheon and kicked the Antis into the anteroom. John Dawson, a young delegate to the Virginia convention, sat in silence for almost the duration, listening to Madison and Henry, Marshall and Monroe. In the final days he took the floor to make his only speech. He aw-shucksed his way through a modest prologue in which he apologized for his diffidence and the "inferiority of my talents" before delivering "my humble opinion" that "had the paper now on your table, and which is so ably supported, been presented to our view ten years ago, (when the American spirit shone forth in the meridian of glory, and rendered us the wonder of an admiring world,) it would have been considered as containing principles incompatible with republican liberty, and therefore doomed to infamy."[113]

Dawson was right.

The Anti-Federalists, it would later be said, were a hodgepodge, a miscellany of malcontents and radicals connected higgledy-piggledy. In fact, the arguments and proposals of Luther Martin, Patrick Henry, and Melancton Smith are far more congruent than those of James Madison, James Wilson, and Alexander Hamilton, who knit a nationalist-federalist crazy-quilt: a suffocating blanket to burke the states. The Antis stood for liberty and self-rule within a small republic. Scale was a paramount concern—which Madison recognized and turned on its head in *The Federalist Papers*, with his ingenious if supportless argument that the largeness, and not smallness, of a polity can be liberty's guarantor. As Michael Lienesch sums up the Antis, "they looked with dread towards big and distant government allied with big and distant economic interests, towards irresponsible or immoral rulers, and towards well-intentioned but weak citizens who would stand by helplessly while their liberties were lost or stolen."[114]

Ring a bell, anyone?

The note of plangency played throughout Martin's Anti-Federal dirge. "[P]owers once bestowed upon a government," he wrote, "should they be found ever so dangerous or destructive to freedom, cannot be resumed or wrested from government but by another revolution."[115]

His Maryland colleague Chase sounded his own note of despond. The people, he said, "are depressed and inactive. They have lost all their former spirit and seem ready to submit to any master." Later, writing to Richard Henry Lee in 1789, he mourned that both government and citizenry had become "monarchical." Chase confessed, "I have the same Affection, and Attachment, as ever, to my Native Country, and her Rights; but for once, in all my life, I despair of the Republic."[116]

Philadelphia's miracle had whipped Maryland's Anti-Federalists.

PART THREE

OF CHASE AND BURR
AND UNMARKED GRAVES

LUTHER MARTIN HAD BET ON THE WRONG HORSE IN 1787, BUT his neighbors did not punish him for it. He would serve thirty years as Maryland's attorney general, which is still the longest such tenure in the state's history. If he had once prosecuted Tories with a patriot's zeal, in his maturity Martin's trials "were always conducted with great fairness to the accused, and the attention of the jury called to the evidence which might operate in his favor as well as that against him."[1] He maintained a busy civil practice, too, most of it in property law.

Martin vowed to accept no position within the government whose creation he had opposed, and he kept that vow. Thus, his post-Philadelphia career is not framed by anglings for appointment. It is, rather, a roiling roundelay of dispute, quarrelsomeness, and dogged adherence to principle.

He was admitted as a counselor to the bar of the Supreme Court of the United States, before which he would argue forty cases, on February 8, 1791, on the motion of U.S. Attorney General Edmund Randolph. How these personages keep crossing paths! It's like a little village, man, as the Martinesque Dan Stuart once croaked. Luther Martin would make ample use of his forensic and declamatory talents before the Court—as he would in matters of blood and the heart, never so lustily as when the character of a forbear of his late wife (Maria had died of cancer in November 1796) was impugned.

Thomas Cresap was a Yorkshire-born Maryland frontiersman who traded with Indians and fought with Indians and speculated in real estate. His contemporaries called him "the Maryland Monster," a "turbulent man" who spoke "horrid Oaths & Imprecations," a disturber of the peace, a damned rascal, and a genial host whose generosity earned him the honorific of "Big Spoon" from the local Indians.[2] Colonel Cresap organized the Maryland Sons of Liberty while in his seventies. (He would live to the age of ninety-six.)

His log home on the Maryland side of the Potomac River, in that jag of land between present-day West Virginia and Pennsylvania, was known as "a haven for travelers" and a backwoods entrepot for fur traders.[3] Luther Martin enjoyed the Cresap hospitality on his ramble through the outback in 1772. Little Maria, six or so years old, granddaughter of Thomas, would reappear in Martin's life, hymeneally, eleven years later.

Thomas's son and Maria's father, Michael Cresap, pushed borders westward habitually, as a charwoman pushes a broom. In one such episode, "Dunmore's War," sometimes known as "Cresap's War," Michael Cresap and associates skirmished with a Mingo war party in the vicinity of the Ohio River. Vengeful whites then massacred the family of a Mingo chief named Logan in spring 1774. The murdered included Logan's mother and sister.

This much is generally agreed upon. (Except by Luther Martin, who denied that Logan was a chief or in any way distinguished, and who called Logan's famed oration "spurious."[4] But we are getting ahead of ourselves.)

Thomas Jefferson, in his *Notes on the State of Virginia*, instanced as a superior example of American Indian oratory the address of Logan to Lord Dunmore. Logan, wrote Jefferson, "who had long been distinguished as a friend of the whites," saw that friendship repaid in blood, when "Col. Cresap, a man infamous for the many murders he had committed on those much-injured people," led a party of whites in slaughtering Logan's family in retaliation for the robbery and murder of two Virginia settlers by a tribe Jefferson identified as "Shawanees." (Most other accounts identified them as Cherokees.)

Jefferson compared Logan's oration to those of Cicero and Demosthenes, and it is tremendously moving. Herewith its conclusion: "Col. Cresap, the last spring, in cold blood, and unprovoked, murdered all the relations of Logan, not sparing even my women and children. There runs not a drop of my blood in the veins of any living creature. This called on me for revenge. I have sought it: I have killed many: I have fully glutted my vengeance. For my country, I rejoice at the beams of peace. But do not harbor a thought that mine is the joy of fear. Logan never felt fear. He will not turn on his heel to save his life. Who is there to mourn for Logan?—Not one."[5]

Michael Cresap, who had died of illness in 1775, had Luther Martin to mourn for him, and to take up arms on his behalf against

Jefferson, too. Martin denied that Michael had killed Logan's family, as Jefferson had broadcast. Oh did he deny it. In a series of open letters to Vice President Jefferson—"a philosopher," Martin jeeringly called him—Michael Cresap's son-in-law discharged a "sacred trust" in debunking this "groundless calumny."[6]

Appearing over several months in 1797–98 in *Porcupine's Gazette*, a Philadelphia Federalist daily published by the guttersnipe William Cobbett, Martin's missives, filled with the author's characteristic blend of invective, incisiveness, and eye-glazing fact-lading surplusage, splatted their mark like a fusillade of birdshot.

The target was inviting. Jefferson wasn't even sure which Cresap he meant to blame. The "Colonel," as Logan via Jefferson identified the homicide, would have been Old Thomas, a preposterous charge. Jefferson must have meant Michael, but Michael's honorific was "the Captain."

Nevertheless, Martin defends Col. Thomas Cresap—"too brave to be perfidious or cruel"—at predictable length.[7] He sneaks in an excellent cheap shot at Jefferson: "The one colonel Thomas Cresap, who, though when the British invaded Virginia, he was more than one hundred years of age, I am confident had he been governor of that state, would not have fled from the seat of his government at least without an attempt to defend it"[8]—a reference to the Federalist-bruited story that Jefferson, as governor, had hightailed it out of Richmond in 1781 when the British attacked. And you wonder why Jefferson hated Martin so!

Jefferson revised his account in 1800 to inculpate Captain Michael, not Colonel Thomas, Cresap. Yet Jefferson had in his possession a 1798 letter from George Rogers Clark, military hero of the western frontier, testifying that Captain Cresap *"was not the author"* (my italics) of the slaughter of Logan's family.[9] Jefferson—perhaps out of a very human reluctance to admit a careless mistake, or maybe because he reciprocated the hatred of Cresap's son-in-law—let the letter molder.

John Dos Passos, with a bias for the Sage of Monticello but an aversion toward hyphens, called Martin "[v]iolently selfrighteous, and with a muleskinner's gift for abusive language,"[10] but one might as justly call him a dutiful son-in-law. His late wife's father and grandfather had been accused of a mass murder that neither committed, and he responded in (un)kind.

I think of him at this stage as a character who might have fit within a Sam Peckinpah Western. A man of violent passions and a multitude of personal sins, yet cleaving to principle and unshakably loyal to friends and family. Jefferson has wronged his father-in-law, so he declares war on Jefferson—with whom he otherwise has much in common, at least in their view of the proper balance between central and local authorities.

Martin was not a petty man given to spite and feuding, but if bee should penetrate bonnet, then watch out, bee! The Jefferson-Cresap imbroglio was a preschoolers' spat compared to Martin's Olympian detestation of Richard Raynal Keene, the bounder who stole his beloved daughter, Eleonora, then just fifteen, and eloped with her to New York City.

Modern Gratitude, first published in 1801 as five letters in the Baltimore *Federal Gazette* and then gathered between two covers the next year, is Martin's 163-page anathema upon the knave. It bears a title hinting of reproachful fuddy-duddyism—the ingratitude of kids these days!—but within, Martin vents prodigious spleen upon poor Keene. The details are perhaps best laid out in a Lifetime Network movie, but as for the passions . . . well, listen to Martin as he kicks it into overdrive:

Had Richard Raynall [sic] Keene, Esq. contented himself with having poisoned the mind and perverted the principles—with having eradicated every sense of duty, and every sentiment of affection to her father, from the heart of a girl of fifteen, who was the joy and pride of that father; had he been satisfied with having forever destroyed her happiness and blasted eternally all her prospects in life, than whom but few of her sex had fairer; nay, had he after this noble achievement been satisfied with circulating the most unfounded falsehood, in order, at my expence, to attempt some little extenuation of the infamy of his conduct, I should most probably have left him, and all the worthless herd, whether in high life or in low, who have been his coadjutors, unnoticed.—And sick as I am, *even at my soul*, with the folly and villainy of mankind, fearless of suffering in the good opinion of those, who really know me, and at this time of life not very anxious concerning the sentiments of others, should have devoted him and the unfortunate victim of his wiles, to experience, at their leisure, all those miseries, with which base ingratitude and filial impiety are not unusually accompanied.[11]

But no, this malign neglect is not possible. Keene has stolen Martin's daughter, dear Eleonora. She is beyond paternal discipline; beyond threats, cajoling, tearful pleas. Martin's only recourse, or so he believes, is vitriol. He uses it.

Briefly: in 1799, Keene, a penniless but enterprising lad with a Princeton education, accepted Martin's kindly offer to read law in his office and board in his home. In early 1801, Martin's two youngest daughters, who had been at school in New York and New Jersey, returned home. Keene continued to read and dine with Martin, but betook his lodging elsewhere. Martin treated Keene almost as a family member, even introducing him to Maryland Governor Ogle.

Eleonora, then fourteen but full of figure, fell under the spell of this Keene, despite Martin's attempts to introduce her into "the most respectable society in America."[12] In June 1801, Keene confessed to his patron that he was smitten with Eleonora. Martin discouraged the match—the mesalliance, in his view, for not only was his daughter too young to plight her troth, but Keene "was not the man whom, I had ever contemplated as the husband of either of my children." They were spoiled girls, used to every indulgence, and while daddy "would infinitely prefer they should marry men of real worth without a shilling, than the richest men in the world destitute of merit," Keene must break off all intercourse with the lass.[13] Withal, should she give birth at a precocious age Eleonora would surely perish, or so feared her father.

Keene pled innocent by reason of passion, but his epistolary self-defense left the father unmoved. "Men must govern and restrain their passions," he lectures Keene, "and keep them within the general rules of morality and rectitude, or they must suffer."[14] (Yes, yes, pharisee, heal thyself.)

Martin reproduces Keene's correspondence in *Modern Gratitude*, strafing it with his own annotations. ("Quite *Jeffersonian*. How great wits will jump!" he exclaims over one oleaginous Keeneism.)[15] Keene's uncles, he spits, have long had their beady eyes on a succession of main chances; he scalds nephew Keene as a gold digger with an eye for barely ripe girls ("I am not the only father whose soul has been tortured by that wretch!"), though he never would have expected his own daughter to suffer Keene's seduction. ("I most certainly should as soon have expected that Miranda in the desart [sic] island could have fallen in love with Calliban.")[16] He even mocks Keene as prose stylist ("turgid, laboured, uphill . . . I cant [sic] read two sentences of Keene's composition, without being out of breath. I would as soon walk from the foot of the Allegany mountain to its summit as to read twenty pages").[17]

"How comes it, Sir, that the objects of your affections always happen to be almost infant children, and children supposed to possess fortune . . . ?" Martin hadn't a fortune, and even if he did, no smooth-talking arriviste was going to marry into it, for "The child that could renounce her father, should forever be by her father renounced."[18] Martin huffs and he puffs, warning that he would "forever disown" his daughter should she marry the wretch.[19] (Disown her, yes; snub her, no. Martin concedes that when encountering the new Mrs. Keene he treats her as any gentleman treats a lady.)

He includes purloined letters from Keene to Eleonora. The lovers, though separated by an obdurate father, maintained a clandestine relationship that doubtless appealed to the young girl's sense of adventure. He proposed in October; she accepted. The intention, claimed Keene, was to endure a torturously long engagement of two years. When the lovers caught wind of a plan to send Eleonora across the Atlantic, Keene intercepted her as she was being hustled off to New York, whence she was to depart for Europe. They married in New York on January 27, 1802. As Keene returned to Baltimore, his betrothed was kidnapped by her father, who demanded that she renounce her new husband else he would exile her to the interior of the country, under guard, until she was twenty-one. "With fluttering hearts, and trembling steps," in Eleonora's words, she escaped with the aid of a kindly intercessor.[20] It must have been terribly exciting for Eleonora to find herself the heroine of her own novel.

Papa Martin dares Keene to challenge him to a duel. "After he has murdered my peace," fumes Luther, "I feel no anxiety as to my person. But if he wishes to add that apex to his crimes, he must assail me in the dark, or behind my back, for one look from me would *wither every nerve in his body!*"[21] Would that Oliver Ellsworth, the lying Landholder, could have been dispatched with the evil eye!

Modern Gratitude is a bizarre performance. If Keene is caned, Martin does himself no credit. The author attributes to nameless friends a question so cogent that he is unable to answer it sufficiently: "[F]or what purpose do you now publish this work? Is he not married to your daughter, do you wish to throw obstacles in the way to his advancement in life? However improperly he may have acted it is now too late to recall the past; and, however undutiful she hath been to you, you certainly will not cast off all parental affection for her—you cannot forget that she is your daughter—and you ought to make great allowance for her extreme youth."[22] The reader, even the Martin partisan, nods in agreement. Let it go, man. Eleonora will die in November 1807, leaving a son named Luther Martin Keene. Forgive her her impetuosity.

Of this he was incapable. He wished upon Keene the ultimate indignity: that he would achieve the position of secretary to Thomas Jefferson.[23] And as for Eleonora, "I ought infinitely rather to have preferred seeing my Eleonora wedded to her grave than to that man."[24] Too soon, she will have consummated both unions.

Modern Gratitude is tiresome, browbeating, nasty: Martin at his worst. Its reader (if any there be!) begins to entertain the Madisonian view of its author. For a time, watching the vials—nay, casks—of scorn pour atop Keene's brash noggin amuses, but good God, Martin, 150 pages of this? Enough, sir, is enough! Alas, not until the 163rd choleric page does Martin announce that "I here throw down my pencil."[25] It's about time!

In June 1802, Keene published in Baltimore a response whose wordiness makes Martin's sentences look Hemingwayesque. Announcing it "my sacred duty to protect" the "offspring of your own loins" against Martin's aspersions,[26] Keene alleges that Martin actually encouraged his suit, and he denies that the blooming Eleonora was anything but a w-o-m-a-n. He begs his father-in-law to desist from this sad spectacle, this pathetic tantrum. But if he had known when to cease he would not have been Luther Martin.

Martin might have taken a lesson or two in pitching woo from the smooth-talking Keene. In 1800–1801, Luther courted a client, the thirty-three-year-old widow Mrs. Mary Magdalina Hager of Washington County, Maryland. A series of embarrassing billets-doux survive the sparking.

"You have a charming little daughter who wants a father. I have two who stand in need of a mother," he writes the widow Hager, resistibly, on May 12, 1800. Do the connubial math, baby! He boasts of his income ($12,000 a year) and his property and promises to make her "a tender, indulgent and affectionate husband." In a subsequent letter his ardor remains strong but his suit is flagging. He has misbehaved, though he admits to no recollection thereof. It is in this letter that he offers the perspiration defense: the "heat of the summer" induces in him a powerful thirst, and if brandy is the only liquid at hand, well, thirst must be quenched. He pledges never again to stagger unless it be with "the intoxication of love!" A Barry White line in a hopeless cause: the Widow Hager rebuffed Martin and married a Colonel Lewis. Always one to have the last word, Luther makes clear that the lovely lady is not the only fish in the sea, informing the coquette that he is going to "look out for some other companion."[27]

He never did find her.

Luther Martin had become Maryland's most vivid character, alternately endearing and infuriating. He walked about with an abstracted air, lost in thought when he was not lost in spirits. He often read as he strode down the street, and it was up to the pedestrians of Baltimore to engage in defensive walking lest they be knocked over. One of the few Martin legends that does not—perhaps—involve bibulousness is that "on one occasion when he accidentally bumped into a cow that had wandered onto Baltimore Street, he tipped his hat, apologized, and continued on his way."[28]

He dressed and was groomed, whether out of defiance or indifference, in a sloppily Federalist style. His long white hair was tied in what I like to think of as a ponytail, giving him the look of an elderly rock-and-roller slipped into shabby gentility. Think Ray Davies as an old man voting red Tory.

He rented a pew at St. Paul's Episcopal in Baltimore from 1800 to 1824, though "he was characteristically ever in arrears for pew rent," and in the final years of his dotage he lost his place. One amused Baltimorean noted that Martin had been known better for "his notorious sacrifices at the shrine of Bacchus" than for any churchly devotions, though Reverdy Johnson recalled that when lodging with Martin on a trip to Annapolis on legal business, the aged attorney burst into his room in the wee hours, lit the darkness with a candle, unpocketed a book, and announced to his drowsy companion, "Young man, I have of late always made it a rule to read a few pages from the book of Common Prayer before going to sleep."[29]

Eyewitness accounts of Martin at the bar do not vary wildly. He was "coarse and gross,"[30] pedantic and long-winded, sedulous and acidulous, and yet altogether—and this must have been alchemic—convincing. He left no precedent unearthed; no divagation unspoken; no auditor unbored. Roger B. Taney, who would go on, as chief justice of the Supreme Court, to commit acts of folly (his gratuitously racist opinion in *Dred Scott*) and courage (his battle against Lincoln's assumption of the power to suspend *habeas corpus*), adjudged Martin "profound" but cuffed him backhandedly with the ungainsayable compliment that "everybody who listened to him would agree that nothing could be added."[31]

"He ordinarily commenced his efforts at the bar with a long, desultory, tedious exordium," according to an 1839 profile. "His address at the bar was not good, nor was his voice agreeable. . . . He was accustomed, from the fashion of the age, to use a considerable quantity of the stimulus of ardent spirit; and we have been credibly informed that he has delivered some of his most powerful and splendid arguments under its strongest excitement."[32]

Joseph Story, the Massachusetts jurist whom James Madison appointed to the U.S. Supreme Court in 1811, wrote a friend in 1808 describing Martin as a "singular compound of strange qualities." Yes! I quote from his perceptive letter at length:

With a professional income of $10,000 a year, he is poor and needy; generous and humane, but negligent and profuse. He labors hard to acquire, and yet cannot preserve. Experience, however severe, never corrects a single habit. I have heard anecdotes of his improvidence and thoughtlessness which astonish me. He is about the middle size, a little bald, with a common forehead, pointed nose, inexpressive eye, large mouth, and well formed chin. His dress is slovenly. You cannot believe him a great man.

Nothing in his voice, his action, his language impresses. Of all men he is the most desultory, wandering, and inaccurate. Errors in grammar, and, indeed, an unexampled laxity of speech, mark him everywhere. All nature pays contribution to his argument, if, indeed, it can be called one; you might hear him for three hours, and he would neither enlighten nor amuse you; but amid the abundance of chaff is excellent wheat, and if you can find it, the quality is of the first order. In the case to which I have alluded, he spoke three days! I heard as much as I could, but I was fatigued almost to death. He did not strike me at all, and if I were to judge solely from that effort, I should say that he was greatly overrated. But every one assures me that he is profoundly learned, and that though he shines not now in the lustre of his former days, yet he is at times very great. He never seems satisfied with a single grasp of his subject; he urges himself to successive efforts, until he moulds and fashions it to his purpose. You should hear of Luther Martin's fame from those who have known him long and intimately, but you should not see him.[33]

One can almost hear Story's crest falling. He is like the disappointed lad who shows up at the ballpark only to watch Mickey Mantle limp to the plate in 1967, Willie Mays misjudge a fly ball as a 1973 Met, Johnny Unitas fumble a snap as a San Diego Charger. You shoulda seen 'em when, kid.

Taney recalled in his memoir his first exposure to Martin, "the acknowledged and undisputed head" of the state's bar. It was during a session of the General Court in Annapolis. Taney, a Catholic Federalist who had been educated abroad, had supped the previous winter on stories of the legends of legal Maryland. His "fox-hunting friends in Calvert County" had told him all about the eminences of the profession. Now, finally, he would see them in the flesh.

"Yet I confess," writes Taney, whose friends had perhaps left out a detail or two in their sketches, "when I first heard Mr. Martin, I was disappointed." Same old Story. "He often appeared in Court evidently intoxicated." His dress lacked the cool style of genteel poverty. He was forgetfully sloppy. His wrists emerged from lace-edged ruffles, very much an old-school Federalist flourish, but his ruffles "were dabbed and soiled, and showed that they had not been changed for a day or more." Sounding the note of the fastidious prig, as if remembering an unpleasant odor, Taney wrote: "His voice was not musical, and when much excited it cracked. His argument was full of digressions and irrelevant or unimportant matter, and his points were mixed up together and argued without order, with much repetition, and his speech was consequently unreasonably long." He was not an ignoramus, conceded Taney, who praised Martin as "an accomplished scholar" who "wrote with classical correctness and great strength." But his speech was hardly fit for the ears of a gentleman. Taney, the planter's son, was horrified that Martin "seemed to delight in using vulgarisms which were never heard except among the colored servants or the ignorant and uneducated whites." He said "cotch" instead of "caught"—as in, "Massa Taney's overseer cotch the runaway slave"—and "sot down" rather than "sat down," as in "Massa Taney sot down and asked his slave to bring him refreshment." (I am being unfair to Justice Taney, who freed his own slaves and followed an admirable jurisprudence of strict construction, except when the peculiar institution was involved.)

Like Story, Taney concluded that Martin was "a profound lawyer," though the qualities constituting that profundity he mentions briefly—"an iron memory,"[34] broad legal knowledge, a fatiguing relentlessness—before complaining that Martin was also a show-off who left no non-germane fact unturned.

Yet he was also "kind to young members of the profession, and liberal, and indeed profuse, in his charities, and easily imposed upon by unworthy objects"[35]—one of whom made off with his beloved Eleonora.

Taney leaves us a story, by way of his posthumous editor Samuel L. Tyler, of Life with Luther. Martin was a master in the intricacies of titles and boundaries and the consequent ejectment suits. He had, after all, fleeced his share of Tories during the war. He took young Taney under his wing in a case to be tried in Hagerstown. The two legists set out from Frederick, twenty-six miles distant. The number calls to mind a marathon, but the only feat of endurance on display was performed by Martin's liver. It seems that the stagecoach stopped every five miles for a relay of horses. Taverns commonly functioned as such waystations, and at every stop Martin drank "whiskey when he could get it, and when he could not, he drank ale, and when he could get neither, he drank buttermilk." A boilermaker with a coat, as a bartender might call it.

They arrived at Hagerstown, Martin not only sheets but veritable volumes to the wind. Since Taney had studied the particulars of the ejectment case at hand and Martin had not, the younger lawyer told his senior that he would stop by his room at eleven that night to rehearse the case. Alas, upon entrance Taney found Martin, fully clad in hat and raiment, though with one boot missing, "lying across the bed, asleep from his various potations on the road and what he had taken since his arrival."

His efforts at awakening the slumbering legal giant were unavailing. Taney returned to his room, agitated, no doubt, that he would have to press the case tomorrow all by himself. When morning came Luther Martin did not present himself, and Taney's knocks on his door failed to rouse him. He would have to take on the formidable opposing counsel, Mr. Shaaff, alone.

"But just as the case was called," writes Tyler, "in walked Mr. Martin; and in none of his forensic efforts did he excel his skill in the management of this cause."[36] Hungover? Bah. It would take more than the hogshead or so of whiskey, ale, and buttermilk he had consumed the day before to throw Luther Martin off his game.

Another story, this one too good to be apocryphal, had Martin accepting a case from a wily client who would pay only if the attorney refrained from drink during the trial. The things people ask of one! Martin could no more stay dry than shut up, but he wanted the case and the fee, so he soaked a loaf of bread in brandy and spent the trial nibbling the staff of life. He won the case, too.[37]

Martin was now an arch-Federalist, though his political views had changed little. State-granted privileges, artificial distinctions, and centralized power he despised in 1787 as well as in 1807 or 1817. But he had never been a leveller or a sentimental democrat, he exalted "well checked, well constituted republicanism" over mob rule,[38] and in his personal detestation of Thomas Jefferson he came to conflate Jacobinism, democracy, despotism, and the hated redheaded polymath of Monticello. Philosophically, he never went over to the Hamiltonian side; the last significant case he argued— *McCulloch v. Maryland*, in 1819—was in defense of states' rights.

His loathing of Jefferson drove him to a Federalism that was so personal, so queerly contoured, fitting as it did the singular shape of Martin, that we can only call it Tertium Quid Federalism. At the bar he defended, consistently, the rights of persons against states and states against the national government, whether in *Mc-*

Culloch v. Maryland or in an 1809 case in which he defended the right to strike of the Journeymen Cordwainers Society of Baltimore, a shoemakers guild.

He was a states' rights Federalist—a rara avis.

It is worth noting that Martin was not the only Anti-Federalist to find a home in the Federalist Party. His Maryland colleague Mercer made the switch during Jefferson's presidency. Judge Robert Yates, the New York delegate who also went home early, dallied with the party of Jay and Hamilton, and the ethically impaired and socially boorish Samuel Chase, who despaired for the Republic upon the Constitution's adoption, apostasized and, like the whore in church, croaked full-throatedly from the Federalist hymnbook. (In fairness, Chase, the parson's son and a devout Episcopalian, was horrified by the atheistic French Revolution and its semi-embrace by the Jeffersonian Republicans.)

Martin never recanted his Anti-Federalism; not for Luther any conspicuous display of Second Thoughts (which tend, in most cases, to be instances of Looking Out for Number One). In 1801 he was quoted in the *Baltimore American* avowing that "from the moment the constitution of the United States was adopted by the requisite number of states until this time, my conduct has been perfectly uniform: from that moment I ceased my opposition to the constitution." Yet though he supported the Washington and Adams administrations, he also pledged never to accept an appointment under the national government, nor to "make my appearance at a presidential levee." He was reconciled to the Constitution, but he would not abase himself before it, or retract a single word he had written in *The Genuine Information*. He continued to believe, even as a Federalist, that "there is too great a tendency in mankind to abuse power."[39]

He would serve as counsel for the defense in two of the great state trials of the early Republic: the Senate trial of Chase, after his impeachment, and the treason trial of Aaron Burr. Both were acquitted, in no small part because of the brilliant defense offered by Martin, despite his having what Albert Beveridge later described as "a face crimsoned by the brandy which he continually imbibed."[40]

Abstemious? No. But the sodden advocate was always ready to take up for friends and bedrock principles—and against Thomas Jefferson.

Samuel Chase had been Martin's benefactor during the Revolution, helping to secure him the position of state attorney general. Like Martin, Chase had been an ardent Anti-Federalist who in the logical course of affairs ought to have been a Jeffersonian Republican but instead developed into a Federalist of hardest crust. Unlike Martin, he lobbied for federal appointment. His repeated supplications paid off in 1796 when this signer of the Declaration of Independence was appointed an associate justice of the Supreme Court by President Washington.

Having lost the executive branch to Jefferson in 1800 (despite desperate machinations that included supporting Aaron Burr when the electoral tie between putative presidential candidate Jefferson and vice presidential candidate Burr threw the choice into the House), and outnumbered in the two chambers of Congress, the Federalists took quarter behind the least democratic branch of the federal government, the judiciary. The federal courts were to be the bulwark of the Federalist resistance to democratic Republicans; they were to act especially as a check on majoritarian or redistributionist impulses in the states. In a colossal act of graceless spoilsportism, President Adams had appointed sixteen Federalists to newly created circuit court judgeships—the "Midnight Judges"—shortly before Adams left office. (The Republicans promptly abolished the positions.)

Randolph's Virginia Plan had provided for lifetime Supreme Court appointments; Hamilton had seconded this quasi-monarchical feature. The Anti-Federalists had foreseen an imperial judiciary, as they prevised so much of what would come to pass. "Brutus" (Robert Yates of New York) wrote, "I question whether the world ever saw, in any period of it, a court of justice invested with such immense powers, and yet placed in a situation so little responsible."[41] These judges, ensconced for life, could strike down any act of the legislature, for reasons capricious, arbitrary, or nefarious. The Federalists had what appeared to be a stranglehold over the federal judiciary; the only way to extricate the country from the grip of overly active Federalist judges was impeachment.

Inspired by Jefferson, the Republicans' first target was a veritable broad side of a barn: John Pickering of New Hampshire, a man lost to madness, drink, or some combination thereof. Pickering was "a friendless, absent, unknown, and imbecile New Hampshire district judge" in Henry Adams's Adamsian formulation.[42] And though insanity was not treason, bribery, high crime, nor misdemeanour, Pickering was impeached in March 1803 and removed from office one year later on a party-line vote.

Pickering had been easy enough pickings; now the Chase was on.

Samuel Chase, the porcine and truculent jurist known as "bacon face,"[43] had made himself an obvious target by his erratic behavior. He became the poster boy for "the callousness and insensitivity to popular opinion that eventually lost political control for the Federalists," writes legal historian Stephen B. Presser.[44] With

Chase's scalp on the wall, Jefferson would seek bigger game—perhaps even Chief Justice John Marshall.*

One of six Supreme Court justices, Chase's duties included "riding circuit" in the federal district courts. Sitting on the Pennsylvania circuit with Judge Richard Peters of the Pennsylvania District Court (who loathed being coupled with the mercurial Marylander), Chase presided over the retrial of John Fries, who had led a namesake rebellion in eastern Pennsylvania against a tax on houses, the revenue from which was needed to pay, in part, for the cost of the suppression of the Whiskey Rebellion. Fries's rebels had freed prisoners from the custody of a federal marshal.

As the trial began, Chase, his memory of previous tax resisters fading as his eminence waxed, distributed his opinion that armed resistance to the execution of the laws of the United States fit the definition of treason—a contested legal point. Chase had pulled the linchpin from the defense's case, and appalled Peters with his injudicious prejudgment. It was, in those early years of the Republic, within the jury's competency to find for both facts and law. Chase had blundered badly. (Chief Justice William Rehnquist would later argue that Chase was merely ahead of his time in asserting that judges decide questions of law and juries consider only questions of fact.)

The final score had been determined before the game had even started. Fries's attorneys withdrew. Chase, though nominally the

---

* Even as a case-hardened Federalist judge, Chase betrayed traces of his earlier Anti-Federalism. In *United States v. Worrall* (1798), in which Robert Worrall was charged with trying to bribe the Commissioner of Revenue to obtain a contract to build a government lighthouse at Cape Hatteras, Chase, drawing breath from the Tenth Amendment, ruled that since Congress had never expressly outlawed the bribery of a revenue commissioner, Worrall had not committed a crime. The next year, in a counterfeiting case involving the same principle, he reached the opposite, Federalist conclusion. Call it growth.

judge, assumed the role of defense counsel, though his "defense" amounted to a piling on of arguments against poor Fries. This would be the first article of his impeachment: that he deprived John Fries of counsel. "Chase's hair-trigger temper, his stubbornness, and his sense of his own judicial prerogative led him to rush precipitously into a confrontation on a sensitive jurisprudential point for which he had little support," writes Stephen B. Presser, who is otherwise not unsympathetic to Chase.[45]

Fries was found guilty; Chase sentenced him to death. (President Adams pardoned him over the protests of his cabinet.)

During the same session in Pennsylvania, Chase had behaved in an intemperate and manifestly unfair manner in the trial of Thomas Cooper, who had been sentenced under the Sedition Act of 1798. Cooper had criticized President Adams for profligacy and militarism, an act of lèse-majesté for which Chase had no tolerance. "If a man attempts to destroy the confidence of the people in their officers . . . he effectively saps the foundation of government," the justice told the jurors.[46] Chase instructed the jury that Cooper was responsible for proving his charges against Adams "beyond a marrow,"[47] a misreading of the Sedition Act (the burden of proof was on the prosecution) and American libel law.

He subsequently mishandled another seditious libel case. Mischievous Luther Martin had given Chase an anti-Adams polemical pamphlet titled *The Prospect before Us* by the scandal-spreader James Callender. Chase, incensed by Callender's histrionic muckspraying, told a Virginia traveling companion aboard a stagecoach that "it is a pity you have not hanged the rascal."[48] When Chase arrived in Richmond to sit at circuit court he attempted to do just that. He convinced a grand jury to charge Callender with violating the Sedition Act.

In *United States v. Callender,* Chase repeatedly stopped Callender's attorneys when they tried to challenge the constitutionality of the sedition law. He taunted and teased them and frequently interrupted midsentence, all the while treating the prosecution with courtesy. Callender was convicted and jailed. Chase's zeal in persecuting the opposition party was so disturbing that federal prison came to be known as "Chase's repository of Republicans."[49]

For his final misstep, on May 2, 1803, Justice Chase instructed a jury in Baltimore of the iniquity of the Republican repeal of Adams's midnight judge appointments and Maryland's recent repeal of property qualifications for suffrage. These portended the rapid destruction of "all protection to property, and all security to personal Liberty; and our Republican Constitution will sink into a *Mobocracy,* the worst of all possible Governments."[50]

Jefferson, upon learning of Chase's outburst, somewhat unctuously asked Rep. Joseph Nicholson of Maryland, "Ought this seditious and official attack on the principles of our Constitution, and on the proceedings of a State, to go unpunished? . . . I ask these questions for your consideration; for myself it is better that I should not interfere."[51] The remedy was obvious. Impeach the bastard.

Federalists feared that Chase, the plumpest target on the court, would be only the first; the real quarry was Chief Justice John Marshall, under whose leadership the federal judiciary was becoming the vanguard of the nationalists.

The House impeached Chase on March 10, 1804, by a vote of 73–32. Eight specific articles of impeachment were drawn up and approved later in the year by comparable margins. They centered on Chase's misconduct in the Fries and Callender cases and threw in his rantings from the Baltimore bench for good measure. (His hamfistedness in the Cooper trial was not cited.) The gravamen of the case was that Chase had operated "in a manner highly arbitrary, oppressive, and unjust."[52]

Richard Henry Lee had adduced as one of his foremost reasons for opposing ratification of the Constitution the weakness of the impeachment clause. Rulers would not fear it; 'twas a paper threat, a bare whisper that was "nothing to them."[53] The test case was in the dock.

Martin, in Philadelphia, had been "strenuous" in favor of judicial appointment by the Senate rather than the executive.[54] And his favored New Jersey Plan would have allowed "State Judiciaries to have Cognizance in the first instance and the Federal Courts to have an Apelant [sic] Jurisdiction only."[55] But bygones were bygone, and now his bête noire, Thomas Jefferson, persecutor of the Cresap name, had targeted his old friend Samuel Chase.

Luther Martin backstopped the defense, a Federalist Dream Team that also included Robert Goodloe Harper, the respected Maryland Federalist; former U.S. attorney general Charles Lee; Joseph Hopkinson of "Hail Columbia" fame ("Sound, sound the trump of Fame! / Let WASHINGTON's great name / Ring through the world with loud applause");[56] and Philip Barton Key, whose nephew composed the poem that bested "Hail Columbia" in the national-anthem sweepstakes.

John Randolph, Black Jack himself, the brilliant Tertium Quid who loved liberty and hated equality, was the chief manager of the seven House prosecutors. Caesar A. Rodney, the Delawarean whose uncle's equestrian feats are immortalized in the musical *1776*, was his most notable colleague.

Was this ever a mismatch.

The Senate trial began February 4, 1805. The senators' desks and benches were covered with crimson cloth; members of the House sat upon benches draped in green fabric. The justices of the Supreme Court were present as spectators, getting a foretaste, perhaps, of their own fates. Eminences packed the galleries. Chief Justice William Rehnquist, who described the scene in *Grand Inquests* (1992), his book on impeachment, was so taken with the pomp of the Chase case (which was modeled on the British impeachment of Warren Hastings, governor-general of India) that it accented his comportment when he presided over the 1999 Senate trial of President Clinton. In the English style, Vice President Burr had ordered Chase to stand throughout his trial, but his wheezing rotundity begged for a chair, and the vice president relented.

Burr, a scrupulously fair presiding officer, barred the senators from coming and going and snacking and roaming as they pleased, giving Martin a captive audience. For once, he did not disappoint.

By all accounts, the House managers stumbled through their presentation in a manner that might charitably be described as unprepossessing. More than fifty witnesses appeared. Those for the prosecution established that Chase was a boor who had it in for radical Republicans, but even if Justice Chase was capricious, rude, and given to occasional errors on the bench, did these flaws—what Henry Adams called "the legality of bad manners"[57]—constitute high crimes and misdemeanors? (Raoul Berger points out, however, that Chase was no equal-opportunity bungler; his errors consistently favored the prosecution.)[58]

Hopkinson led off for the defense, speaking effectually to the Fries-related article, but the auditors were there to hear Luther Martin, who was the fourth of Chase's attorneys to speak. The

Senate gallery was packed. Martin spoke for five hours on Saturday, February 23, refreshed only by modest quantities of wine and water, and as he had done in notable addresses before, he needed another day to conclude. So on the following Monday he delivered two more hours of his patented dense yet diffuse oratory.

"Our property, our liberty, our lives can only be protected by independent judges," lectured Martin.[59] Unleashing his sarcasm, which he seldom bothered to keep leashed in any event, Martin ridiculed the prosecution for making much of an allegedly supercilious bow that Chase had made to Callender attorney William Wirt. And of Chase's injudicious use of the word *damned*, Martin remarked that south of the Susquehanna River the curse is "connected with subjects the most pleasing: thus we say indiscriminately a very good or a damned good bottle of wine, a damned good dinner, or a damned clever fellow."[60]

The galleries guffawed. In seven hours that were not without their moments of longueur, Martin had trivialized the case against Chase and convincingly depicted the judge as a wronged man, a martyr to an independent judiciary, an aged patriot being garroted by scoundrels. The Pennsylvania lawyers he had insulted were deserving of his jibes. After all, they were Pennsylvania lawyers. (Senator William Plumer, the statesmanlike New Hampshire Federalist, recorded in his diary that "Mr. Martin really possesses much legal information & a great fund of good humor—keen satire & poignant wit. He is far from being a graceful speaker. His language is often incorrect—inaccurate, & sometimes is too low. But he certainly has *talents*.")[61]

Caesar Rodney gamely replied to Martin that judges, like kings, were not infallible, and Randolph, expatiating behind a strange variety of facial contortions and moues and even sobs, belittled

Chase as only Black Jack could ("haughty, violent, imperious . . . a timid poltroon").[62]

The Senate voted on Friday, March 1. Vice President Burr, enjoying the gravity of it all, announced that "the Sergeant-at-Arms will face the spectators and seize and commit to prison the first person who makes the smallest noise or disturbance."[63]

The heavily Republican Senate (twenty-five of thirty-four members) delivered a rebuke to the impeachers. Only three of the eight articles attracted a majority of the thirty-four senators, and none received the requisite two-thirds vote. One article received a resounding zero votes. The highest vote for removal was nineteen votes, on Article VIII, concerning Chase's diatribe before the Baltimore grand jury.

Chase's acquittal was a signal event in judicial history. As Rehnquist writes, "it assured the independence of federal judges from congressional oversight of [their] decisions,"[64] and it removed impeachment as a potent threat to the independence of federal judges.

Was this Luther Martin's finest hour? I think not. For sheer desperate arduousness and sloppy genius, nothing beats his summer of '87 and the subsequent speech to the Maryland legislature and publication of *The Genuine Information*. But the Chase defense has come down to us as Martin's brief shining moment, thanks to Henry Adams, who called him "the rollicking, witty, audacious Attorney-General of Maryland; boon companion of Chase and the whole bar; drunken, generous, slovenly, grand; bulldog of federalism, as Mr. Jefferson called him; shouting with a school-boy's fun at the idea of tearing Randolph's indictment to pieces and teaching the Virginia democrats some law,—the notorious reprobate genius, Luther Martin."[65]

This is the single best passage ever written about Martin; you can almost sense Adams loosening his collar, forgetting his grief, and wishing that he could knock back a few brandies with the bulldog.

Adams had a parti pris against Randolph, of whom he sneers that "he knew no more law than his own overseer." (The dig, always the dig, against the slaveowner.) Randolph's opening address he dismisses as showy, a mere flash without afterglow. Martin's speech, by contrast, is marked by "rugged and sustained force; its strong humor, audacity, and dexterity; its even flow and simple choice of language, free from rhetoric and affectations; its close and compulsive grip of the law; its good-natured contempt for the obstacles put in its way."[66]

This is in such stark contradistinction to the usual account of a Martin address that one wonders if it is the product of Henry Adams's sapience or the fact that, for once, Luther Martin found himself on the correct side of history, or should we say the side that historians have taken: that of judicial independence. Had he descanted for many hours on the splendor of the Virginia Plan in June 1787 might his speech have been recorded not as a soporific mess but as a tour de force of Federalist wisdom? It makes me wonder.

Martin took no fee in the Chase case. You can't charge a friend, especially when he sets you up to whip the philosopher of Monticello.

Chase did not forget Martin's valiant defense. In later years, Martin, by now thoroughly mannerless and frequently reprimanded, appeared drunk before the Federal Circuit Court in Baltimore. The district judge sought to persuade Justice Chase to sign a commitment for contempt of court against Martin, but Old Bacon Face demurred, saying "whatever may be my duties as a judge,

Samuel Chase can never sign a commitment against Luther Martin."[67]

Not that Martin never offered provocation. In 1810, Clarkson and Jett relate, Martin stumbled drunkenly through an insurance case before Justice Chase. "I am surprised that you can so prostitute your talents," Chase reproved him. "Sir," replied Martin, grin no doubt creasing his mouth, "I never prostituted my talents except when I defended you and Colonel Burr"—and here he turned to the jury, certainly with a wink—"a couple of the greatest rascals in the world."[68]

With "better breeding and redemption from habits of inebriety his [Martin's] would be a perfect character," assessed Aaron Burr,[69] whose remarks on character might be taken with a grain, or beach, of salt. For the vice president who had presided so solemnly over the trial of Samuel Chase had killed Alexander Hamilton six months previous (on July 11, 1804) in a duel that Hamilton had brought upon himself by whispering the vilest scurrilities about the cagey, cultured, but apparently incorrupt Burr.

Burr is the grievous angel in Martin's twilight sky, so perhaps we had better meet him, checking our social-studies textbook prejudices at the cover.

Aaron Burr, only son of the union between the second president of the College of New Jersey and the daughter of Jonathan Edwards, was orphaned at age two, but not before his mother had taken his measure: "Aaron is a little dirty Noisy Boy . . . very Sly and mischievous. He had more sprightliness than [sister] Sally & most say he is handsomer, but not so good tempered. He is very resolute & requires a good Governor to bring him to terms."[70]

Just so, Mother! No good governor ever did bring him to terms, though the Calvinist God of his pious parents may have eventually had something to say about the matter. Burr enrolled at the College of New Jersey in 1769 at age thirteen, just missing Luther Martin. (Burr joined the Cliosophic Society, which Martin had helped to found.) He began a lifelong practice of writing letters in cipher, which habit was later to cast a veil of mystery over even his innocent epistles. As a character in Gore Vidal's *Burr* says, "He makes even a trip to the barber seem like a plot to overthrow the state."[71]

Aaron Burr is the damned of the founding generation. He was a gallant young lieutenant-colonel at Valley Forge. A rake, plotter, roue, bankrupt, murderer. For such a slick operator he had bad timing. As Charles Beard wrote, "Burr fixed his eyes on the Southwest too soon. Had he come on the scene many years later, he might have won immortality in American history, with Sam Houston and Davy Crockett."[72] Anent his famous duel, we must concede that poor Burr made a ghastly mistake in slaying Alexander Hamilton . . . twenty years too late.

Burr was a Republican who "continually flirted with the Federalists,"[73] and in fact Luther Martin had publicly supported Burr's dubious claim to the presidency in 1800–1801, when the election was thrown into the House after Burr and Jefferson tied in the Electoral College.

The ever optimistic Burr was suffering through the year of his nadir in 1804 when James Wilkinson, whom he had known in the Revolution, renewed their acquaintance. Burr's term as vice president was coming to an end; he had been passed over for a second term in favor of the elderly George Clinton. He had lost a bitter race for governor of New York. He had killed his foul libeller Alexander Hamilton and barely escaped prosecution for the act in New York and New Jersey. He was finished as a politician.

Wilkinson, a Maryland native, a young brigadier general of the Revolution (he fought alongside Benedict Arnold), was a Mississippi River trader, a traitor, an epaulet-draped blowhard, friend of freebooters and filibusterers, and a host celebrated for his open-bar policy. He was general-in-chief of the U.S. Army and the St. Louis–based appointed governor of the upper Louisiana Territory. The French prefect in New Orleans dismissed him as "a flighty, rattle-headed fellow, often drunk, who has committed a hundred impertinent follies."[74] Ever alert for side action, General Wilkinson had taken a secret oath of allegiance to Spain in 1787 and been in that nation's pay since. Plotting with Burr to take Mexico was thus a betrayal of two countries, but a man had to look out for number one, didn't he?

In the spring of 1805, Burr undertook the journey that was to make his name a byword for traitor. He visited with the stunning Margaret Blennerhassett on Blennerhassett Island in the Ohio River near present-day Parkersburg, West Virginia (her husband Harman was not at home; uncharacteristically, Burr wished the husband were there); with his warm admirer Andrew Jackson in Nashville; with General Wilkinson at Fort Massac on the Ohio; and then on he went to New Orleans, where he charmed that city's French, Spanish, and American grandees. Burr's western tour brought him to St. Louis and Vincennes before he recrossed the Appalachians in November. Having been expelled from the ruling class of one country, he had mapped his next country.

Despite Burr's penchant for secrecy, tongues wagged so furiously that by summer 1805 diplomats and packet-boat captains alike knew that something was up. On August 4, British Minister (the U.S. didn't merit an ambassador) Anthony Merry wrote Lord Mulgrave, British foreign secretary, that whether through indiscretion or betrayals, public reports circulated that "a convention is to be called immediately from the States bordering on the Ohio and Mississippi for the purpose of forming a separate government."[75] Two days later Merry informed the foreign office that Mr. Burr had offered his assistance to His Majesty's Government in effecting "a separation of the Western part of the United States from that which lies between the Atlantic and the mountains, in its whole extent."[76] All he wanted was an advance of half a million dollars.

Murk covers the plot to this day, but Burr in his mischief seems to have planned something like this: raise an army of backwoodsmen, mercenaries, and disgruntled officers, the adventurous and the ambitious, to take Mexico from Spain; seize New Orleans; and detach the western states and territories from the United States. These would be united under the benevolent leadership of Aaron Burr. This mid-American empire would range from New Orleans to Tennessee, from Kentucky to West Florida to Texas. Or maybe not. Even at two centuries' distance Burr is inscrutable. As the author of one of the most recent accounts of the Burr conspiracy concludes, "Burr might have been out to take Mexico; he might have been after New Orleans; he might have been targeting Florida . . . he might even have wanted to capture Washington, as bizarre as that sounds; or he might have been planning various combinations of these things. We shall never know."[77]

Blennerhassett Island was the base of operations, an insular storage site for boats, provisions, and comestibles. Its eponym was a credulous, purblindly nearsighted immigrant who lived in magnificent isolation with his lovely young wife—who was also his sister's daughter, an incestuous conjugation that explains their exile.

Of Harman Blennerhassett Henry Adams sniffed, "Of all the eager dupes with whom Burr had to deal, this intelligent and accomplished Irish gentleman was the most simple."[78] Burr missed Harman on his first visit to the island, but he drew him into his web by flattering him that "I have considered your seclusion as a fraud on society."[79] Blennerhassett, something of a reclusive poly-math, had literary ambitions, which he fulfilled by publishing a series of essays in the *Ohio Gazette* under the pen name "Querist," in which he argued for western independence.

Disunion was in the air. Timothy Pickering, Massachusetts Federalist, spoke of severance. Within the next decade, New Eng-landers—chafing under a federal government whose executive was seemingly given in perpetuity to Virginia; dismayed by westward expansion and the consequent inevitability of their region's dimin-ished national clout; appalled by Jefferson's commerce-strangling embargoes and Madison's pointless War of 1812—would seriously entertain breaking away from the United States. If the sons of Bunker Hill and Concord could consider separation, why not the traders and men of Kaintuck and western Virginia, whose ties to the political and financial capitals of the East Coast were tenuous at best? And if healthy republics were impossible beyond a certain size, what exactly was wrong with a trans-Appalachian republic? (Nothing—except its dubious paternity. Burr and Wilkinson seemed to have in mind an empire. Their quest was for glory and gold, not liberty and self-rule. And besides, timing is all. When Sam Houston, Davy Crockett, and associates liberated Texas from Mexico, Burr, anticipating Charles Beard, exulted, "You see? I was right! I was only thirty years too soon! What was treason in me thirty years ago, is patriotism now!")[80]

For her assistance, England was to receive "a decisive preference in matters of commerce and navigation," according to Jonathan Dayton, the former New Jersey Federalist senator, Constitutional

Convention delegate, and Burr co-conspirator.[81] When the English balked at funding the Burr revolution, Dayton approached the Spanish, who also declined to subsidize an insurrection (though Burr expected a bloodless revolution).

Burr was to set up his presidency, or kingship, in New Orleans. Wilkinson would be second-in-command. But the general, whether to save his own skin or simply because treachery is the nature of the treacherous, turned on Burr. He informed Jefferson of the plot and in blunderbuss fashion executed an undeclared martial law on New Orleans. Rumors ran riot in the Crescent City that Burr and an army of thousands, black and white, revolting slaves and savage brigands, were on their way to visit bloodbath and conquest upon the city. In reality, the man who would be emperor was travelling down the Mississippi with a flotilla of about ten boats and one hundred men and women. He caught wind of Wilkinson's betrayal en route and surrendered January 17, 1807, north of Natchez. Two weeks later he escaped, donning a beaver hat and a boatman's pantaloons, but was soon caught and sent on to Richmond.

As Blennerhassett Island was within John Marshall's jurisdictional ambit, the chief justice presided over the trial of the new century in the House of Delegates chamber in Richmond. Black Jack Randolph, whom Martin had bested in the Chase trial, was foreman of the grand jury.

Burr was indicted for treason, as were Blennerhassett and five other alleged cabalists. The Constitution (Article III, Section 3) establishes that "Treason against the United States, shall consist only in levying war against them, or in adhering to their enemies, giving them aid and comfort. No person shall be convicted of treason unless on the testimony of two witnesses to the same overt act, or on confession in open court." It is the only crime mentioned therein, and the specificity of the language repudiates the looser "constructive treason" under which rebels in Europe had been executed.

Where, in re Burr, was the overt act? Or the two witnesses? The "overt act" was a December 1806 assemblage on Blennerhassett Island, from which Burr was absent, being in Kentucky at the time. The sum of armaments among these insurrectionists was "a half-dozen rifles . . . and a few fowling pieces."[82]

Burr pled not guilty, denying that separation by force was ever his intent. He was merely leading a party to scout the Bastrop land grant along the Ouachita River in Louisiana as a prelude to its colonization. Besides, he was far from the scene of the alleged treason: Blennerhassett Island, where in the summer and fall of 1806 boats, ammunition, and provisions for the expedition were assembled.

George Hay, U.S. district attorney for Virginia and James Monroe's son-in-law, led the prosecution, assisted by William Wirt and the acerbic Virginia Lieutenant Governor Alexander McRae. As in the Chase trial, the imbalance was pronounced, though Wirt delivered a prolegomenon of such lush floridity that the speech was given a name ("Who is Blennerhassett?") and place of honor in schoolhouse recitations. In any case, Jefferson was "the leading counsel in the prosecution of Aaron Burr," as Albert Beveridge wrote,[83] feeding Hay arguments, precedents, and strategy via urgent missives.

In Burr's corner were some of the bar's leading lights: John Wickham, able Richmond barrister; Edmund Randolph, he of the Virginia Plan and also Washington's secretary of state and first attorney general; Benjamin Botts, an able attorney of the Old Dominion; a lame legist named Jack Baker, who was considered "a jolly dog";[84] Charles Lee, President Adams's attorney general; and Luther Martin.

Martin, writes a Burr biographer, was "the spearhead of Burr's forensic army, the vituperative bludgeoner, the tickler of ground-lings."[85] Leave the careful construction of the case, the marshalling of facts, to John Wickham; Luther Martin would sic the hated Jefferson.

"Lawyer Brandy-Bottle" winged Jefferson whenever possible. Adverting to the president's reluctance to produce documents (army and navy orders and the Jefferson-Wilkinson correspondence) that the defense believed would exonerate Burr, he snarled, "whoever withholds necessary information that would save the life of a person charged with a capital offense is substantially a murderer and so recorded in the register of heaven."[86]

Cresap will be avenged!

Chief Justice Marshall ordered Jefferson to produce himself and the requested papers in court. Jefferson, asserting an early form of executive privilege, refused. "He is no more than a servant of the people," roared Martin in republican objection.[87]

Two mighty streams met in confluence—Martin's hatred of Jefferson and his indignation at the mistreatment of his friend Burr—and produced the roar of a Niagaran cataract. "The President has undertaken to prejudge my client by declaring that 'of his guilt there can be no doubt,'" he began his declamation. "He has assumed the knowledge of the Supreme Being himself, and pretended to search the heart of my highly respected friend. He has proclaimed him a traitor in the face of that country which has rewarded him. He has let slip the dogs of war, the hell-hounds of persecution, to hunt down my friend."[88] The Federal Bulldog snarled, ready for the dogfight.

The affair shows Jefferson at his most vindictive. In June 1807, he wrote George Hay,

> Shall we move to commit Luther Martin as *particeps criminis* with Burr? Graybell [a Baltimore merchant] will fix upon him misprision of treason at least. And at any rate, his evidence will put down this unprincipled and impudent federal bull-dog, and add another proof that the most clamorous defenders of Burr are all his accomplices. It will explain why Luther Martin flew so hastily to the "aid of a friend," abandoning his clients and their property during a session of a principal court in Maryland, now filled, as I am told, with the clamors and ruin of his clients.[89]†

Jefferson seemed always just behind the curtain, yanking the prosecutorial strings. He had overplayed his hand; Burr had misstepped, but *treason*? Martin wasted no opportunity to spray him with obiter dicta, such as his observation that the president "was of no celebrity as a lawyer before the Revolution, and he has since been so much engaged in political pursuits that he has had time enough to unlearn the little law he ever knew."[90]

Folklore has it that Martin made clumsy suit for Burr's ravishing and married daughter, Theodosia. "Especially did she make a

---

† Charles Beard wisely reminds us that "the bench mark from which to survey Jefferson's career is not the Burr Conspiracy" (Beard, "Introduction," *The Aaron Burr Conspiracy*, xi). Besides, Jefferson raged but did nothing to quiet Martin. Jefferson did avoid the humiliation of a courtroom examination by Luther Martin when he defied the subpoena to testify. Yet the Jefferson of the Burr prosecution was hardly the secession-accepting Jefferson who had written to Dr. Joseph Priestley on January 29, 1804, "Whether we remain in one confederacy, or form into Atlantic and Mississippi confederacies, I believe not very important to the happiness of either part" (Thomas Jefferson to Joseph Priestley, January 29, 1804, *The Jefferson Cyclopedia*, 794).

conquest of the elderly and bibulous, but redoubtable, Luther Martin," writes Nathan Schachner in his *Aaron Burr* (1937), though Clarkson and Jett dismiss such rumors as a "good deal of nonsense." Theodosia, whom Burr had educated with equal parts rigor and love, was by all accounts a young woman of extraordinary attainment. In the words of Nathan Schachner, one of Burr's best biographers:

> She was beautiful with a proud lift of head and an aristocratic mold of features; wherever she went half the eligible young males of the town sighed fruitlessly after her—and a good many of the older, more substantial men, too. She was beloved equally by women as by men. She was "elegant without ostentation, and learned without pedantry." She danced "with more grace than any young lady of New York." Her wit sparkled and warmed; she possessed her father's airy sense of humor. She was the living proof of the success of Aaron Burr's seemingly repellent system of education.[91][‡]

Martin was not above enlisting widows and orphans in his pleas to the jury. Referring to the shrewd and brilliant and desirable and sexually knowing Theodosia, he expressed the devout wish to be successful "in wiping away the tear of filial piety and in healing deep wounds inflicted on the breast of a child." Adams refers to this as "almost passionate,"[92] but then Clover could tell us about his blind spots in that respect.

At all events, James Wilkinson, pompous and pathetic, made a poor peg on which to hang a case. John Randolph called him "the

---

‡ Theodosia, wife of South Carolina Governor Joseph Alston, would perish at sea when the pilot boat on which she was travelling—the *Patriot* by name, carrying not only Theodosia but also the plunder of a privateer—disappeared in a storm off the coast of Cape Hatteras in the final hours of 1812.

only man that I ever saw who was from the bark to the very core a villain."[93] No sentient jury would convict a man on Wilkinson's word.

Martin's concluding speech stretched for fourteen hours over—does this ring a bell?—two days. He fortified himself with occasional slurps of rum. The coolly logical Burr thought it too zealous.

On August 31, Chief Justice Marshall defined for the jury *treason* in such a manner as to make Burr's acquittal inevitable. Marshall ruled for once as a strict constructionist, his apostasy perhaps explained by antipathy toward Jefferson. The accused must "truly and in fact levy war" against the United States, explained Marshall.[94] Dreaming of the conquest of Mexico, talking up secession in Kentucky, and floating toward New Orleans with a few dozen poorly armed settlers fell outside the definition. Was force employed against the state? Were there two witnesses, physically present, who had seen Burr in the act of treason? The Constitution meant what it said: it could not be used as an iron maiden to discipline renegade politicians or personal enemies of the president.

On September 1, the prosecution rested. The jury deliberated quickly and returned with what William Rehnquist called a "very strange form of verdict":[95] "We of the jury say that Aaron Burr is not proved to be guilty under this indictment by any evidence submitted to us. We therefore find him not guilty."

Not quite a rousing declaration of innocence, but still. Burr was cleared of treason. Martin had once again bested Jefferson. (Give opposing attorney Wirt credit for hitting his mark during one of the anti-climactic post-acquittal hearings. When Martin, presented with an edited letter, huffed, "We take no extracts," Wirt cracked, "Unless it be of molasses.")[96]

Harman Blennerhassett kept a diary during the trial and its sequelae. Therein we find a frank, conflicted, but ultimately warm portrait of Luther Martin—"the rear-guard of Burr's forensic army." He descants and he decants, he expatiates and he expectorates. Blennerhassett all but blurts "Yuck!" at the "preternatural secretion or excretion of saliva which embarrasses [Martin's] delivery." The attorney is described as awkward, disgusting, coarse, fulsome, gross, crude, and ungrammatical.[97] He "bears everything to an extreme," he is indefatigable, he fills taverns with spit-flecked animadversions upon Jefferson, astonishing feats of memory and recitation, and acts of a drunkard's kindness. He tries Burr's patience but he "worships even [Burr's] vices."[98]

He is perpetually in his cups, once disabled by "yesterday's morning potation," yet he is one "of the best hearted men alive." (Martin, Anti-Federalist heart still beating under the Federalist skin, praises one of Blennerhassett's secessionist essays.)[99]

In November 1807, while staying in Baltimore, Blennerhassett, Burr, and Martin (as well as Chief Justice Marshall) were threatened with the gallows in handbills that warned *"Lawyer* Brandy-bottle" and his associates that they, or at least their effigies, were to be hanged at three in the afternoon. A mob of 1,500 surrounded Martin's home on Charles Street. Tar and feathers were among the mob's weapons, and although the effigies dangled, the only damage done was by the rocks that crashed through Martin's windows. It was a long night. The crowd was acting as if to fulfill the July 4 toast drunk to Martin in Elkton, Maryland: "May his exertions to preserve the Catiline of America procure him an honorable coat of tar, and a plumage of feathers, that will rival in finery all the mummeries of Egypt."[100] To which the redoubtable Martin later replied, as Pilate might have:

[L]et me inquire who is this gentleman whose guilt you have pronounced, and for whose blood your parched throats so thirst? Was he not, a few years past, adored by you next to your God? . . . He was then in power. He had then influence. . . . Go, ye holiday, ye sunshine friends—ye time servers—ye criers of ho-sanna to-day and crucifiers to-morrow—go hide your heads, if possible, from the contempt and detestation of every virtuous, every honourable inhabitant of every clime.[101]

The Burr acquittal was Martin's last great victory. No doubt the jeers for his triumph grimly amused him.

—

There's not enough whitewash in the world to wipe Luther Martin clean for hagiography. Allow me to direct your attention to another damned spot. In September 1810, he denounced Judge John Scott of the Criminal Court of Baltimore County for a color-blind appli-cation of habeas corpus. The custom, sanctioned by Maryland law, had been for constables to pick up itinerant Negroes suspected of being runaway slaves. The presumption was that they were bonds-men: the detained had to offer proof of free status, else they were condemned to servitude.

In July 1810, the judge heard the case of a Negro woman named Nancy Thompson. Speaking for her confinement was none other than that Honorary-Counselor of the Maryland Society for pro-moting the Abolition of Slavery et al., Luther Martin, who knocked off a two-day, six-and-a-half-hour discourse (with refreshment) on why Nancy Thompson should be presumed enslaved. Judge Scott, having no reason other than her skin color to believe her a slave, released Nancy. All hell—or, rather, Luther at his most Luciferian—broke loose.

Martin published an open letter to the justices of the peace and constables of Baltimore County, warning that "we may expect the slaves of the southern states to flee to the city of Baltimore as a city of refuge where they shall be safe from the claims of their masters." Murders, thefts, break-ins, and general hooliganism would wrack the city. He called upon the constables to do their duty: "whenever they meet with a negro or mulatto, whom they do not know to be free, and who has not such certificate of his freedom as the law requires . . . immediately take him up as a runaway, and carry him before a justice of the peace." He offered his legal services, pro bono, to any constable who did so.

This is hard to square with Martin the precocious abolitionist. We might say that in making the law his life, Martin had subordinated his conscience to the criminal code. Or perhaps, as with Jefferson, Keene, and so many others who had crossed him, Martin wished to flog Judge Scott with the closest weapon at hand. "Humanity & Law," writing in *The Scourge*, said of Martin: "All who know him, well know that he habitually clamours against every judge who has the independence to decide against him. His infallibility must not be questioned. And those who have the hardihood to question it, are deemed by him either knaves or fools."[102]

Whatever the goad in this instance, it tarnishes the luster on Martin's statue of liberty.

Two of Luther and Maria's children died early. Their eldest daughter, Juliet, had been married in 1799 to a New York merchant named Hector Scott.[103] Eleonora, youngest of the three surviving sisters, eloped so spectacularly. The other Martin daughter, Maria, who had tried to thwart Eleonora's elopement, also married a Keene, by coincidence, the unrelated naval officer Lawrence Keene. They separated, and she would spend years in a Philadelphia asylum, victim of a "religious mania." Paul Clarkson located several letters (dated 1815–16) from Martin to Dr. Thomas Parke, attending physician at the hospital. They make for heartbreaking reading. Maria, "my dear unhappy Child," had fastened upon "gloomy horrid Ideas of our God & Saviour."[104] To wit: that the Creator, "instead of being a God of goodness & mercy, . . . is a cruel tyrant delighting in misery of which he is the Author."[105]

Martin requests that Maria be kept apart from the other unfortunates in the hospital, lest their pathetic states confirm her bleak suspicions. But he rebuffs Dr. Parke's suggestion that Maria be released to "a Matron kind yet firm."[106] Maria would know no consolation, it seems, nor even freedom of movement, short of her death.

Martin's insistence upon Maria's confinement seems monstrous, though I suppose we ought not be too comminatory without staggering a mile in his shoes.

If things had never quite been together for Luther Martin, now they were falling apart. Nothing held. His sight was blear; his mood, dolor. He still had moments of supreme competency, but more and more, the words no longer came in any meaningful sequence.

In *Fletcher v. Peck* (1810), Martin was "so drunk," as one judge told historian Henry P. Goddard, "that the Court adjourned rather than let him attempt to conduct his case."[107] He ran for the Maryland House of Delegates in 1811 and came in last in a three-way race. By 1812, Joseph Story, now a Republican-appointed associate justice of the Supreme Court, was confiding to a friend that Martin, appearing before the court in *Le Roy v. The Maryland Insurance Company*, was "heavy, unmethodical, and inaccurate."[108]

For two years (1814–16) he served as Chief Judge of the Court of *Oyer and Terminer* in Baltimore city and county until this criminal court was abolished by the state legislature. Improbably, he resumed his attorney generalship, which he had resigned in 1805 after twenty-seven years in the office. A biblical forty years after his first appointment, he reprised his role in 1818, serving four years as a racked and spectral figure. He bestirred himself to one more battle: *McCulloch v. Maryland* (1819), in which this Anti-Federalist turned arch-Federalist argued the Anti-Federalist (if pro-federalism) position that Maryland had the right to tax the Baltimore branch of the Second Bank of the United States. He was a shadow of his former self, delegating much, and though he rose from his brandy-marred dotage to offer an Anti-Federalist-tinged interpretation of the Constitution, this decisive battle would go to the Hamiltonians.

Daniel Webster represented the bank along with two Marylanders: Attorney General William Wirt and the exquisite dandy and erstwhile Anti-Federalist William Pinkney. Representing Maryland were Martin and Joseph "Hail Columbia" Hopkinson, his co-counsel in the Chase defense.

It was in this setting that Webster remarked that the "power to tax involves, necessarily, a power to destroy," which Chief Justice Marshall would rephrase slightly and wind up with the credit for. Over the course of nine days the justices would hear a concatenation of forensic gems. Joseph Story later called Pinkney's address the greatest speech he had ever heard.

Luther Martin, for the last time, would revisit in his remarks to the Court the Philadelphia convention of thirty-two summers ago. He began, according to court reporter Henry Wheaton, with lections from *The Federalist Papers* and the Virginia and New

York ratifying conventions. "[I]t was then maintained," Martin informed his juniors,

> by the enemies of the constitution, that it contained a vast variety of powers, lurking under the generality of its phraseology, which would prove highly dangerous to the liberties of the people, and the rights of the States, unless controlled by some declaratory amendment, which should negative their existence. This apprehension was treated as a dream of distempered jealousy. The danger was denied to exist: but to provide an assurance against the possibility of its occurrence, the Tenth Amendment was added to the constitution.

The amendment's simple guarantee that "The powers not delegated to the United States by this Constitution, nor prohibited by it to the States, are reserved to the States respectively, or to the people," merely restated the frequent assurances of the Madison party.

But after thirty years, the mask had fallen off. The real face of the beast was visible. "We are now called upon," marveled Martin, "to apply that theory of interpretation which was then rejected by the friends of the new constitution, and we are asked to engraft upon it powers of vast extent, which were disclaimed by them, and which, if they had been fairly avowed at the time, would have prevented its adoption."[109]

Had the Philadelphia delegates of 1787 or the state convention delegates of 1788 known that a state would have been constitutionally barred from taxing a national bank—that is, had they listened to Luther Martin—the Constitution would have been roundly and rightly rejected. But it was too late now.

The Court—unanimously—ruled that the federal government had the power to charter the bank (which President Madison had signed into existence in 1816) and that states may not tax such an "instrument" of the United States. In expressing the latter opinion Marshall relied on Luther Martin's own supremacy clause—that bastard offspring of the language he had substituted for Madison's negative in Philadelphia. No compromise, it seems, goes unpunished.

Chief Justice Marshall brushed aside Maryland's assertion that the Constitution originated with the states. After all, there was that preamble: We the People. Gouverneur Morris's artful rewrite strikes again! Strict constructionists can't say Sam Adams, Patrick Henry, and Luther Martin didn't warn them.

Martin's loss in *McCulloch v. Maryland* was seeded in 1787. Once the Constitution had been adopted, it was in the order of things that state taxation of a national institution would be proscribed. As Marshall declared in his magisterial opinion, the federal government "is the government of all; its powers are delegated by all; it represents all, and acts for all. . . . The nation, on those subjects on which it can act, must necessarily bind its component parts."[110] Creating a national bank was within the powers of the federal government; so was proscribing state taxation thereof. The defeat of the states was total, complete, shattering. Nationalism had triumphed.

Marshall's rhetoric flew upwards and beyond, out of the empyrean and into the imperial. "Throughout this vast republic," he rhapsodized, "from the St. Croix to the Gulf of Mexico, from the Atlantic to the Pacific, revenue is to be collected and expended, armies are to be marched and supported. The exigencies of the nation may require that the treasure raised in the north should be transported to the south, that raised in the east conveyed to the west, or that this order should be reversed."[111] The only limits upon this strapping young nation were those imposed by God, and even these were hard to descry. Expand. Expand. Expand. Territorially, administratively, judicially. The sky was the limit. It was just as Luther Martin had predicted. *The Genuine Information* turned out to be genuine after all.

The implied powers that Marshall had found between the lines of those enumerated had a balloon-like potential for growth. As the Virginia agrarian theorist and U.S. Senator John Taylor of Caroline would write in 1820, *McCulloch* had established that "Congress may pass any internal law whatsoever in relation to things, because there is nothing with which war, commerce and taxation may not be closely or remotely connected."[112] *McCulloch*, concluded Leonard W. Levy, "laid the constitutional foundations for the New Deal and the Welfare State."[113]

James Madison might complain that *McCulloch v. Maryland* "convert[ed] a limited into an unlimited Government,"[114] but he was thirty years late in making the argument. Madison, like Martin, opined that the document would never have been ratified had the delegates to Philadelphia and the state conventions known how the Marshall Court was going to interpret those emanations and penumbras. This was a disingenuous argument for the father of the national negative to make. His 1787 plan would have all but effaced the states!§

As for the elderly Martin, "His vast learning," lamented Roger B. Taney, "was hidden in the oblivious darkness of an extinguished intellect."[115] What alcohol had not numbed was polished off by a

---

§ Let us dream for a moment. Perhaps if Martin's defense of Justice Chase had been tipsy and unsure and unsuccessful, the emboldened Jeffersonians really would have gone after Marshall, and therefore . . . ahh, as William Riker knew, *What If?* is a wonderfully intoxicating game.

severe stroke. The light had gone out but the motor ran still. His old friends averted their eyes; the young bucks at the bar regarded him with pity or contempt.

Henry P. Goddard, writing in 1887, relates a story told by a venerable member of the Baltimore bar. The place was the U.S. District Court at Baltimore; the opposing counsels were Roger B. Taney and William Wirt, whose paths crossed Martin's so many times. The year was in the early 1820s.

The "court room was filled with interested auditors," writes Goddard,

> when suddenly there was a little ripple of excitement and the crowd gave way to right and left as a grey-haired old man tottered into the room, and passing inside the rail seated himself as if accustomed to the place. Apparently ignoring or unconscious of the deference shown him by the lawyers present, as well as by the spectators, he seemed absorbed in munching a piece of gingerbread. The old gentleman had on well-worn knee breeches, yarn stockings, silver buckles on his shoes and ruffles on his shirt bosom and sleeves. It needed but brief observation to satisfy the surprised young lawyer that the old man was nearly bereft of mental power and had wandered into the court room more from a feeble instinct than with any real purpose.[116]

In such manner did Luther Martin spend his final years.

Yet in the slough of senility Martin was paid an unprecedented and unrepeated honor: the state of Maryland levied a tax on her lawyers in order to defray the expenses of a penniless old man who had been "so generous, and withal so improvident."

Enacted by the Maryland legislature in February 1822, when Martin was in his seventy-fifth year, the joint resolution provided that "each and every practitioner of law in this State shall be and he is hereby compelled . . . to obtain from the Clerk of the County Court in which he may practise, a license to authorize him so to practise, for which he shall pay annually . . . the sum of five dollars." The "proceeds raised by virtue of this resolution" are for "the use of Luther Martin . . . [T]his resolution shall cease to be valid at the death of the said Luther Martin."[117]

This is not the tribute a state pays to its bums or even entertaining gadflies. Maryland, at least, recognized Luther Martin's substance.

A quarter-century earlier, Martin had "fondly flattered myself" that his daughter Eleonora would "strew with flowers the paths of my declining life."[118] But she was long in the grave. Where might a feeble, addled, and lonely old toper turn?

To a traitor, of course.

Aaron Burr, in gratitude for Martin's 1807 defense, would take in the decrepit Anti-Federalist. The descendant of Jonathan Edwards had once remarked that Martin's "heart is overflowing with the milk of benevolence."[119] Burr remembered Martin's kindness, his courage in standing up for the rights of a despised outcast. In return, Burr gave Martin shelter when he had no home.

"About the only good thing I know of Colonel Burr," wrote Roger B. Taney, "is, that . . . he took Mr. Martin to his house and provided for his wants, and took care of him until his death."[120]

The end drew near. Senile, reduced by drink and age to a babbling old man dressed in threadbare and lost on the streets of Burr's New York, "a discrowned, demented and almost friendless Lear" was Luther Martin.[121]

Luther Martin died on July 10, 1826, six days after Jefferson and Adams had passed in magnificent simultaneity. No one suggested that the timing of Martin's death had anything to do with the divine. Members of the bench and bar of Baltimore, regretting the passing of "the Patriarch of the Profession,"[122] wore mourning for thirty days. Martin was buried in Manhattan, in the St. John's Cemetery of Trinity Church. He probably never had a stele to mark his grave, but in any event Manhattan is built on destruction, on the effacement of the past, and so in 1895 the city purchased the land for a park. In 1946, it was paved over, and a year later it was named for the corrupt dead mayor James J. "Beau James" Walker.

A few months ago I was in the Vampire City promoting my latest book at 2 a.m. on a radio talk show along with a fourth-rate comedian named Jackie the Jokeman and his stripperish consort. Oh, how we have elevated public discourse in the 220 years since Luther Martin unburdened himself of heretical opinions in Philadelphia!

I wished on my recent visit that I might pay my respects to Mr. Martin, but God only knows where lie his mortal remains. He has no stone. No monument. His grave is unmarked. Paved over. His was the path not taken, the path that led to . . . liberty? Peace? Chaos? We'll never know.

I suppose my obvious agreement with much of what Martin said removes from me the handiest and hoariest of conservative objections to so many acts of the national government: namely, "It's unconstitutional!" The Anti-Federalists would have told you that such "unconstitutional" interventions were inevitable. Indeed, they are not so much unconstitutional as they are logical extensions of the consolidationist thought of Madison, Wilson, Morris, and the nationalist faction that triumphed at Philadelphia.

You cannot "prop up a dangerous and defective system by *great names*," protested Martin, vainly.[123] The Constitution, identified so strongly with Madison, Washington, and Franklin, has been unassailable since birth. Even Beard's bearding left it unscratched. Maybe it's time for a renewal of the antinationalist campaign that failed with Paterson's New Jersey Plan in June 1787.

(That said, I hasten to add that I would much rather live under a government limited to the functions described in the U.S. Constitution than as a subject of the runaway American Empire of the early-twenty-first century.)

But as we survey the minatory contours of the U.S. government and see a powerful central state involved in perpetual warfare around the globe, a tax-gathering apparatus with its grip on every paycheck, states and localities reduced to mere administrative units of the central state, this Anti-Federalist suspects that for all his vices, for all his inability to shut the hell up, for all the gallons upon gallons of rotgut he imbibed, Luther Martin was not a reprobate, but a prophet.

NOTES

Introduction: The People Who Lost

1. In 1976, William Appleman Williams, groping toward a means of realizing a decentralized socialism, wrote that "we must move another step into the Past beyond Madison. Unlike Lincoln, we must seek to honor rather than to supersede our revolutionary forefathers. That means evoking and using the Past to create a Future that honors our primary commitment to self-determination. We must return therefore to the Articles of Confederation. That document offers us a base from which to begin our voyage into a human Future; a model of government grounded in the idea and the ideal of self-determined communities coming together as equals when and as it is necessary to combine forces to honor common values and realize common objectives." William Appleman Williams, *America Confronts a Revolutionary World: 1776–1976* (New York: William Morrow, 1976), 184.

2. Cecilia Kenyon, editor, *The Antifederalists* (Indianapolis: Bobbs-Merrill, 1966), cvi.

3. Robert Allen Rutland, *The Ordeal of the Constitution: The Antifederalists and the Ratification Struggle of 1787–1788* (Norman, OK: University of Oklahoma Press, 1966), vii.

4. "Cato V," *New York Journal*, November 22, 1787, in *Essays on the Constitution of the United States*, edited by Paul Leicester Ford (Brooklyn: Historical Printing Club, 1892), 265.

5. Robert Yates, *Secret Proceedings and Debates of the Convention Assembled at Philadelphia, in the Year 1787, for the Purpose of Forming the Constitution of the United States of America* (Richmond: Wilbur Curtiss, 1839), 178. The speaker was James Wilson.

6. "Agrippa IV," *Massachusetts Gazette*, December 3, 1787, in *Essays on the Constitution of the United States*, 65.

7. Quoted in Louie M. Miner, *Our Rude Forefathers: American Political Verse, 1783–1788* (Cedar Rapids, IA: Torch Press, 1937), 204.

8. Samuel Adams to Richard Henry Lee, December 3, 1787, in *The Writings of Samuel Adams, 1778–1802*, Vol. 4, edited by Harry Alonzo Cushing (New York: Putnam's, 1908), 324.

9. Jonathan Elliot, editor, *The Debates in the Several State Conventions on the Adoption of the Federal Constitution*, Vol. 3 (Philadelphia: J. B. Lippincott, 1836), 44.

10. Herbert J. Storing, *What the Anti-Federalists Were* For (Chicago: University of Chicago Press, 1981), 48.

11. Samuel Bannister Harding, *The Contest Over Ratification of the Federal Constitution in the State of Massachusetts* (Cambridge, MA: Harvard University Press, 1896), 40.

12. "Philadelphiensis," February 7, 1788, in Kenyon, *The Antifederalists*, 72.

13. James Madison, *Notes of Debates in the Federal Convention of 1787 Reported by James Madison* (Athens, OH: Ohio University Press, 1984 [1840]), 240.

14. Wendell Berry, "The Mad Farmer Manifesto: The First Amendment," in *Collected Poems, 1957–1982* (San Francisco: North Point, 1985), 154.

15. Michael Lienesch, "In Defence of the Antifederalists," *History of Political Thought*, Vol. 4, No. 1 (February 1983): 80.

16. Harding, *The Contest Over Ratification of the Federal Constitution in the State of Massachusetts*, 77.

17. Quoted in Philip A. Crowl, "Anti-Federalism in Maryland, 1787–1788," *William and Mary Quarterly*, Vol. 4 (1947): 464.

18. *Saturday Bulletin*, January 9, 1869, 1, 4, Maryland Historical Society Library, Pamphlet 11508.

19. Ashley M. Gould, "Some Incidents in the Life of Luther Martin," address to the Maryland State Bar Association, July 9, 1903, Maryland Historical Society Library, Pamphlet 4744.

20. Max Farrand, editor, *The Records of the Federal Convention of 1787*, Volume III (New Haven, CT: Yale University Press, 1911), 93.

21. Samuel L. Tyler, *Memoir of Roger Brooke Taney* (Baltimore: John Murphy & Co., 1872), 66.

22. Forrest McDonald, *We the People: The Economic Origins of the Constitution* (Chicago: University of Chicago Press, 1965 [1958]), 70.

23. Max Farrand, *The Fathers of the Constitution* (New Haven, CT: Yale University Press, 1921), 116.

24. Max Farrand, *The Framing of the Constitution of the United States* (New Haven, CT: Yale University Press, 1913), 36–37.

25. Clinton Rossiter, *1787: The Grand Convention* (New York: Macmillan, 1966), 250.

26. Catherine Drinker Bowen, *Miracle at Philadelphia* (Boston: Little, Brown, 1966), 40, 119.

27. Henry Goddard, *Luther Martin: The "Federal Bull-Dog"* (Baltimore: Maryland Historical Society, 1887), 34.

28. Jean Fritz, *Shh! We're Writing the Constitution* (New York: Putnam's, 1987), 26.

29. M. E. Bradford, *Founding Fathers: Brief Lives of the Framers of the United States Constitution*, 2nd edition (Lawrence, KS: University of Kansas, 1994), 110.

30. William H. Rehnquist, *Grand Inquests: The Historic Impeachments of Justice Samuel Chase and President Andrew Johnson* (New York: Morrow, 1992), 23.

31. Gore Vidal, *Burr* (New York: Bantam, 1974 [1973]), 464.

32. Everett D. Obrecht, "The Influence of Luther Martin in the Making of the Constitution of the United States," *Maryland Historical Magazine*, Vol. 27, No. 3 (September 1932): 289.

33. Farrand, *The Records of the Federal Convention of 1787*, Vol. 3, 295.

Part One: The Philadelphia Story

1. Quoted in William Safire and Leonard Safir, *Good Advice on Writing: Great Quotations from Writers Past and Present on How to Write Well* (New York: Simon & Schuster, 1992), 126.

2. Paul S. Clarkson and R. Samuel Jett, *Luther Martin of Maryland* (Baltimore: Johns Hopkins Press, 1970).

3. Luther Martin, *Modern Gratitude*, in five numbers (Baltimore, 1802), 131.

4. Ibid., 132.

5. Ibid., 133.

6. Ibid., 137.

7. Ibid., 134.

8. Ibid., 135.

9. Ibid., 138.

10. Ibid., 140.

11. Luther Martin, "To the Public," August 19, 1779 (Baltimore: M. K. Goddard), 1, Maryland Historical Society Library, Broadside 87.

12. Luther Martin, "An Address to Robert Lemmon, Esq.," November 22, 1779 (Baltimore: M. K. Goddard), 5, Maryland Historical Society Library, Rare MF 179.

13. James Herring, editor, *The National Portrait Gallery of Distinguished Americans*, Volume IV (Philadelphia: James B. Longacre, 1839), 7.

14. Martin, *Modern Gratitude*, 146.

15. Ibid., 151.

16. Clarkson and Jett, *Luther Martin of Maryland*, 36.

17. Thomas Paine, *Common Sense*, in *The Life and Major Writings of Thomas Paine*, edited by Philip S. Foner (Secaucus, NJ: Citadel Press, 1974/1948 [1776]), 4.

18. Clarkson and Jett, *Luther Martin of Maryland*, 37–38.

19. Tyler, *Memoir of Roger Brooke Taney*, 70–71.

20. Goddard, *Luther Martin: The "Federal Bull-Dog,"* 37.

21. "Luther Martin," *Dictionary of American Biography*, Volume VI (New York: Scribners, 1961 [1935]), 345.

22. *The National Portrait Gallery of Distinguished Americans*, 2.

23. Obrecht, "The Influence of Luther Martin in the Making of the Constitution of the United States," *Maryland Historical Magazine*: 179.

24. Philip A. Crowl, *Maryland During and After the Revolution: A Political and Economic Study* (Baltimore: Johns Hopkins Press, 1943), 48–50, 128.

25. Ibid., 89.

26. Farrand, *Records of the Federal Convention of 1787*, Vol. 3, 14.

27. Albert Jay Nock, *Our Enemy, the State* (New York: Morrow, 1935), 159, 165.

28. "The Articles of Confederation and Perpetual Union," in Merrill Jensen, *The Articles of Confederation: An Interpretation of the Social-Constitutional History of the American Revolution, 1774–1781* (Madison: University of Wisconsin Press, 1966 [1940]), 263.

29. Jensen, *The Articles of Confederation*, xxii.

30. Ibid., 124.

31. Ibid., 239, 244.

32. Ibid., 3.

33. Elliot, *The Debates in the Several State Conventions,* Vol. 4, 271.

34. Elliot, *The Debates in the Several State Conventions*, Vol. 3, 140–41.

35. James Madison to Edmund Randolph, February 25, 1787, in *The Debates in the Several State Conventions*, Vol. 5, 106.

36. John Fiske, *The Critical Period of American History, 1783–1789* (Boston: Houghton Mifflin, 1916 [1888]), vi–vii.

37. Peter S. Onuf, "Maryland: The Small Republic in the New Nation," in *Ratifying the Constitution*, edited by Michael Allen Gillespie and Michael Lienesch (Lawrence, KS: University Press of Kansas, 1989), 180.

38. Quoted in Jensen, *The Articles of Confederation*, 197.

39. Onuf, "Maryland: The Small Republic in the New Nation," 176.

40. Crowl, *Maryland During and After the Revolution*, 37.

41. Ibid., 22.

42. James Haw, Francis F. Beirne, Rosamond R. Beirne, and R. Samuel Jett, *Stormy Patriot: The Life of Samuel Chase* (Baltimore: Maryland Historical Society, 1980), 2.

43. Ibid., 112.

44. Publius Letters I, II, and II, *The Papers of Alexander Hamilton, 1768–1778*, Vol. 1, edited by Harold C. Syrett (New York: Columbia University Press, 1961), 563, 568, 582.

45. Quoted in Henry Mayer, *A Son of Thunder: Patrick Henry and the American Republic* (New York: Grove, 2001 [1992]), 370.

46. Frank Greene Bates, "Rhode Island and the Formation of the Union," *Columbia University Studies in History, Economics and Public Law*, Vol. 10, No. 2 (1898): 159.

47. Madison, *Notes of Debates in the Federal Convention of 1787*, 23.

48. Quoted in Charles Warren, *The Making of the Constitution* (Boston: Little, Brown, 1929), 17–18.

49. "Luther Martin's Reply to the Landholder," March 19, 1788, Farrand, *Records of the Federal Convention*, Vol. 3, 294.

50. Madison, *Notes of Debates in the Federal Convention of 1787*, 28.

51. Luther Martin, "The Genuine Information," Farrand, *Records of the Federal Convention*, Vol. 3, 191.

52. Quoted in Warren, *The Making of the Constitution*, 137.

53. Thomas Jefferson to George Hay, June 19, 1807, *The Jefferson Cyclopedia*, Vol. 2, edited by John Foley (New York: Russell & Russell, 1967 [1900]), 542.

54. Goddard, *Luther Martin: The "Federal Bull-Dog,"* 16.

55. Luther Martin Before the Maryland House of Representatives, November 29, 1787, Farrand, *Records of the Federal Convention*, Vol. 3, 152.

56. William H. Riker, *The Strategy of Rhetoric: Campaigning for the American Constitution*, edited by Randall L. Calvert, John Mueller, and Rick K. Wilson (New Haven, CT: Yale University Press, 1996), 20, 148.

57. Irving Brant, *James Madison: Father of the Constitution, 1787–1800* (Indianapolis: Bobbs-Merrill, 1950), 23.

58. Farrand, *The Framing of the Constitution of the United States*, 16.

59. "A Letter of His Excellency, Edmund Randolph, Esq.," October 10, 1787, in Elliot, *Debates in the Several State Conventions*, Vol. 1, 491.

60. Madison, *Notes of Debates in the Federal Convention of 1787*, 31.

61. James Madison to Edmund Randolph, April 8, 1787, in Elliot, *Debates in the Several State Conventions*, Vol. 5, 108.

62. Yates, *Secret Proceedings and Debates of the Federal Convention*, 101.

63. Madison to Randolph, April 8, 1787, Elliot, *Debates*, Vol. 5, 107.

64. Charles F. Hobson, "The Negative on State Laws: James Madison, the Constitution, and the Crisis of Republican Government," *William and Mary Quarterly*, Series 3, Vol. 36, No. 2 (April 1979): 215. For a reading of Madison that stresses his federalism, see Lance Banning, *The Sacred Fire of Liberty:*

James Madison and the Founding of the Federal Republic (Ithaca, NY: Cornell University Press, 1995).

The negative was not Madison's first brainstorm on dealing with insubordinate states. As a new member of Congress in 1781, Madison had sponsored an amendment to the Articles permitting Congress "to employ the force of the United States as well by sea as by land to compel the States to fulfill their federal engagements" (Hobson: 220–21). Banning de-emphasizes—unsuccessfully, to my mind—the coercive cast of this amendment, noting that at least Madison wasn't a loose constructionist relying on implied powers. Banning, *The Sacred Fire of Liberty*, 20–22.

65. Brant, *James Madison*, 49. No man crosses Jemmy Madison and escapes the ire of Irving Brant. To Martin he ascribes the desire "to tear Virginia to pieces" (66) as well as to protect his debt-ridden cronies in the Samuel Chase faction.

66. Christopher Collier and James Lincoln Collier, *Decision in Philadelphia: The Constitutional Convention of 1787* (New York: Random House, 1986), 116.

67. Clarkson and Jett, *Luther Martin of Maryland*, 84.

68. "Luther Martin's Reply to the Landholder," March 14, 1788, Farrand, *Records of the Federal Convention*, Vol. 3, 283.

69. Madison, *Notes of Debates in the Federal Convention of 1787*, 105.

70. Bowen, *Miracle at Philadelphia*, 247.

71. Farrand, *Records of the Federal Convention*, Vol. 3, 88.

72. "Biographical Sketch," in Yates, *Secret Proceedings and Debates of the Federal Convention*, 329.

73. James Madison to Edmund Randolph, March 11, 1787, Elliot, *Debates*, Vol. 5, 106.

74. "Letter from the Hon. Robert Yates and the Hon. John Lansing, Jun., Esquires," n.d., Elliot, *Debates*, Vol. 1, 480–81.

75. Quoted in Bowen, *Miracle at Philadelphia*, 106.

76. Farrand, *Records of the Federal Convention*, Vol. 3, 90.

77. Quoted in Staughton Lynd, "Abraham Yates's History of the Movement for The United States Constitution," *William and Mary Quarterly*, Vol. 20, No. 2 (April 1963): 223–25. Lynd notes that Abraham Yates "was a decentralist who believed in weak government and a propertied middle class": 230.

78. Madison, *Notes of Debates in the Federal Convention of 1787*, 204.

79. Farrand, *The Framing of the Constitution of the United States*, 60.

80. "Biographical Sketch," in Yates, *Secret Proceedings and Debates of the Federal Convention*, 333.

81. Farrand, *Records of the Federal Convention*, Vol. I, xviii.

82. Madison, *Notes of Debates in the Federal Convention of 1787*, 117.

83. Farrand, *The Framing of the Constitution of the United States*, 89.

84. Quoted in John E. O'Connor, *William Paterson: Lawyer and Statesman, 1745–1806* (New Brunswick, NJ: Rutgers University Press, 1979), 11.

85. Ibid., 137. Paterson's biographer emphasizes his subject's nationalism and conjectures that he cooperated with Anti-Federalists only because he would take his small-state allies where he could find them. The New Jersey Plan, in this account, "was simply intended as a stalking horse for equal representation" (149). Luther Martin sure didn't think so. Then again, Martin was "obstreperous" (151) and did not orate but rather "exploded" (152).

86. Yates, *Secret Proceedings and Debates of the Federal Convention*, 118.

87. *The Delegate from New York or Proceedings of the Federal Convention of 1787, from the Notes of John Lansing, Jr.*, edited by Joseph Reese Strayer (Princeton, NJ: Princeton University Press, 1939), 53.

88. Yates, *Secret Proceedings and Debates of the Federal Convention*, 131.

89. Madison, *Notes of Debates in the Federal Convention of 1787*, 125–26.

90. Ibid., 129.

91. Yates, *Secret Proceedings and Debates of the Federal Convention*, 141.

92. Lansing, *Proceedings of the Federal Convention of 1787*, 65.

93. Madison, *Notes of Debates in the Federal Convention of 1787*, 134.

94. Yates, *Secret Proceedings and Debates of the Federal Convention*, 145.

95. Madison, *Notes of Debates in the Federal Convention of 1787*, 135.

96. Yates, *Secret Proceedings and Debates of the Federal Convention*, 145.

97. Quoted in Alfred F. Young, "The Framers of the Constitution and the 'Genius' of the People," *In These Times* (September 9–15, 1987): 12.

98. Madison, *Notes of Debates in the Federal Convention of 1787*, 142, 146.

99. Yates, *Secret Proceedings and Debates of the Federal Convention*, 149.

100. Madison, *Notes of Debates in the Federal Convention of 1787*, 148.

101. William H. Riker, "What If Elbridge Gerry Had Been More Rational and Less Patriotic? (1787)," in *What If? Explorations in Social-Science Fiction*,

edited by Nelson Polsby (Lexington, MA: Lewis Pub. Co., 1982), 15–16. Professor Riker wrote a really fine two-act play about the Constitutional Convention. As far as I know, "Mr. Madison and Mr. Morris" has yet to be produced. Calling all impresarios . . .

102. Warren, *The Making of the Constitution*, 233.

103. Yates, *Secret Proceedings and Debates of the Federal Convention*, 151.

104. Bradford, *Founding Fathers*, xviii.

105. Jackson Turner Main, *The Antifederalists: Critics of the Constitution 1781–1788* (Chapel Hill, NC: University of North Carolina Press, 1961), xi.

106. Elliot, *Debates*, Vol. 2, 224.

107. Martin, "The Genuine Information," Farrand, *Records of the Federal Convention*, Vol. 3, 192.

108. Ibid., 194.

109. Ibid., 192.

110. Madison, *Notes of Debates in the Federal Convention of 1787*, 159.

111. Martin, "The Genuine Information," Farrand, *Records of the Federal Convention*, Vol. 3, 224.

112. "Luther Martin's Reply to the Landholder," March 19, 1788, Farrand, *Records of the Federal Convention*, Vol. 3, 291.

113. Madison, *Notes of Debates in the Federal Convention of 1787*, 159.

114. Yates, *Secret Proceedings and Debates of the Federal Convention*, 155–56.

115. Madison, *Notes of Debates in the Federal Convention of 1787*, 201–3.

116. Yates, *Secret Proceedings and Debates of the Federal Convention*, 187–91.

117. Lansing, *Proceedings of the Federal Convention of 1787*, 87–90.

118. Tyler, *Memoir of Roger Brooke Taney*, 66–67.

119. Ibid., 65.

120. Madison, *Notes of Debates in the Federal Convention of 1787*, 205–6.

121. Ibid., 209–10.

122. Ibid., 131.

123. Collier and Collier, *Decision in Philadelphia*, 93, 118.

124. Madison, *Notes of Debates in the Federal Convention of 1787*, 78.

125. Ibid., 104.

126. Yates, *Secret Proceedings and Debates of the Federal Convention*, 150–51.

127. Bowen, *Miracle at Philadelphia*, 111. I am afraid that on a recent trip to Philadelphia, our daughter Gretel and I mugged disrespectfully at Wilson's

grave outside Christ Church. Emboldened by our display of Anti-Federalist lèse-majesté, we next brandished images of Andy Jackson (on paper twenty-dollar bills, alas!) in front of the Bank of the United States. Take that, Nicholas Biddle!

128. Quoted in Rutland, *The Ordeal of the Constitution*, 27.

129. Quoted in Brant, *James Madison: Father of the Constitution, 1787–1800*, 26.

130. Madison, *Notes of Debates in the Federal Convention of 1787*, 240–41. Morris spoke on the last day that Yates kept notes. Yates, whose records of the 5th are desultory, does not quote from the speech. Morris is unwittingly making the case that, since Americans are by habit so mobile, sovereign states, crossconnected by numerous familial and social ties, would be unlikely to war against one another. Thanks to Jeremy Beer for this insight.

131. Martin, "The Genuine Information," Farrand, *Records of the Federal Convention*, Vol. 3, 190.

132. Madison, *Notes of Debates in the Federal Convention of 1787*, 217.

133. Yates, *Secret Proceedings and Debates of the Federal Convention*, 203.

134. Madison, *Notes of Debates in the Federal Convention of 1787*, 220–21.

135. Yates, *Secret Proceedings and Debates of the Federal Convention*, 212.

136. Ibid., 213.

137. Madison, *Notes of Debates in the Federal Convention of 1787*, 230–31.

138. Ibid., 241–42.

139. Yates, *Secret Proceedings and Debates of the Federal Convention*, 218.

140. Ibid., 221.

141. Madison, *Notes of Debates in the Federal Convention of 1787*, 238.

142. Luther Martin, "The Genuine Information," Farrand, *Records of the Federal Convention*, Vol. 3, 190.

143. Ibid., 188.

144. Ibid., 183.

145. Ibid., 185.

146. Madison, *Notes of Debates in the Federal Convention of 1787*, 289–90.

147. "The Landholder," February 29, 1788, Farrand, *Records of the Federal Convention*, Vol. 3, 273. If this was an olive branch to the nationalists, write Clarkson and Jett, it was a "far greater concession to the larger states than they had ever been willing to make to their smaller sisters." *Luther Martin of Maryland*, 114.

148. Madison, *Notes of Debates in the Federal Convention of 1787*, 305–6.

149. "Luther Martin's Reply to the Landholder," March 19, 1788, Farrand, *Records of the Federal Convention*, Vol. 3, 287.

150. Martin, "The Genuine Information," Farrand, *Records of the Federal Convention*, Vol. 3, 206.

151. "Luther Martin's Reply to the Landholder," March 19, 1788, Farrand, *Records of the Federal Convention*, Vol. 3, 287.

152. Elliot, *Debates*, Vol. 3, 539.

153. Madison, *Notes of Debates in the Federal Convention of 1787*, 304–5.

154. Martin, "The Genuine Information," Farrand, *Records of the Federal Convention*, Vol. 3, 203.

155. Madison, *Notes of Debates in the Federal Convention of 1787*, 305.

156. Hobson, *William and Mary Quarterly*: 216–18.

157. Madison, *Notes of Debates in the Federal Convention of 1787*, 304.

158. Ibid., 88.

159. Charles Beard, *An Economic Interpretation of the Constitution of the United States* (New York: Free Press, 1986 [1913]), 127.

160. Letter to Jefferson from ?, October 11, 1787, Farrand, *Records of the Federal Convention*, Vol. 3, 104.

161. George Washington to Alexander Hamilton, July 10, 1787, in ibid., 56.

162. Farrand, *Records of the Federal Convention*, Vol. 2, 191–92.

163. Daniel Carroll to James Madison, May 28, 1788, in Farrand, *Records of the Federal Convention*, Vol. 3, 306.

164. James McHenry to Daniel Carroll, January 9, 1788, in ibid., 320.

165. Gordon Wood, *Revolutionary Characters: What Made the Founders Different* (New York: Penguin, 2006), 50.

166. Forrest McDonald, *E Pluribus Unum: The Formation of the American Republic, 1776–1790* (Indianapolis: Liberty Press, 1979 [1965]), 296.

167. Madison, *Notes of Debates in the Federal Convention of 1787*, 481–82.

168. Ibid., 214.

169. Ibid., 515.

170. Ibid., 316.

171. Ibid., 459.

172. Ibid., 493.

173. Ibid., 474.

174. Ibid., 497.

175. Warren, *The Making of the Constitution*, 575.

176. Madison, *Notes of Debates in the Federal Convention of 1787*, 502.

177. Ibid., 268.

178. Luther Martin Before the Maryland House of Representatives, November 29, 1787, Farrand, *Records of the Federal Convention*, Vol. 3, 156.

179. Madison, *Notes of Debates in the Federal Convention of 1787*, 502–5.

180. Ibid., 553–57.

181. Ibid., 566.

182. "Objections of the Hon. George Mason to the Proposed Federal Constitution," Elliot, *Debates*, Vol. 1, 494–96.

183. Madison, *Notes of Debates in the Federal Convention of 1787*, 488.

184. Martin, "The Genuine Information," Farrand, *Records of the Federal Convention*, Vol. 3, 227.

185. "Luther Martin's Reply to the Landholder," March 19, 1788, Farrand, *Records of the Federal Convention*, Vol. 3, 288.

186. Madison, *Notes of Debates in the Federal Convention of 1787*, 564.

187. "Luther Martin's Reply to the Landholder," March 19, 1788, Farrand, *Records of the Federal Convention*, Vol. 3, 292.

188. Rossiter, *1787: The Grand Convention*, 240.

189. Martin, "The Genuine Information," Farrand, *Records of the Federal Convention*, Vol. 3, 180–81.

190. "Letter Containing the Reasons of the Hon. Elbridge Gerry, Esq., for Not Signing the Federal Constitution," Elliot, *Debates*, Vol. 1, 493.

191. Farrand, *Records of the Federal Convention*, Vol. 2, 649.

192. Ibid., Vol. 3, 93.

193. "Luther Martin's Reply to the Landholder," March 19, 1788, Farrand, *Records of the Federal Convention*, Vol. 3, 294–95.

194. Madison, *Notes of Debates in the Federal Convention of 1787*, 566.

195. Farrand, *Records of the Federal Convention*, Vol. 3, 85.

Part Two: Maryland, My Maryland;
Or, Luther Martin's Theses

1. Quoted in Warren, *The Making of the Constitution*, 631–32.

2. Richard Henry Lee to General John Lamb, June 27, 1788, *The Letters of Richard Henry Lee*, Vol. 2, edited by James Curtis Ballagh (New York: Macmillan, 1914), 475.

3. Elliot, *Debates*, Vol. 2, 250.

4. Quoted in Bowen, *Miracle at Philadelphia*, 269. For Lee on the national negative, see J. Kent McGaughy, *Richard Henry Lee of Virginia: A Portrait of an American Revolutionary* (Lanham, MD: Rowman & Littlefield, 2004), 189–90.

5. "Luther Martin's Reply to the Landholder," March 19, 1788, Farrand, *Records of the Federal Convention*, Vol. 3, 287.

6. Quoted in Lienesch, "In Defence of the Antifederalists," *History of Political Thought*: 70. Lienesch calls the Antis "conservative reformers."

7. Elliot, *Debates*, Vol. 4, 93.

8. Elliot, *Debates*, Vol. 3, 522.

9. Ibid., 137.

10. Kenneth M. Stampp, "The Concept of a Perpetual Union," *Journal of American History*, Vol. LXV, No. 1 (June 1978): 11.

11. Elliot, *Debates*, Vol. 3, 22.

12. Martin, "The Genuine Information," Farrand, *Records of the Federal Convention*, Vol. 3, 195.

13. J. Thomas Scharf, *History of Maryland, From the Earliest Period to the Present Day* (Baltimore: John B. Piet, 1879), 540.

14. Samuel Bryan, "Centinel No. 14," *The Letters of Centinel: Attacks on the US Constitution 1787–1788*, edited by Warren Hope (Ardmore, PA: Fifth Season Press, 1998), 82.

15. "Luther Martin Before the Maryland House of Representatives," November 29, 1787, Farrand, *Records of the Federal Convention*, Vol. 3, 151.

16. Martin, "The Genuine Information," in ibid., 173.

17. Ibid., 174.

18. Ibid., 177.

19. Ibid., 178.

20. Ibid., 186.

21. Ibid., 178.

22. Ibid., 180–81.

23. "Luther Martin Before the Maryland House of Representatives," November 29, 1787, Farrand, *Records of the Federal Convention*, Vol. 3, 152.

24. Martin, "The Genuine Information," in ibid., 203.

25. Ibid., 179–80.

26. Ibid., 196–97.

27. Ibid., 215.

28. Ibid., 204.

29. Elliot, *Debates*, Vol. 3, 29–30.

30. Martin, "The Genuine Information," Farrand, *Records of the Federal Convention*, Vol. 3, 205.

31. Ibid., 214.

32. Ibid., 223–24. Goddard writes, "It was from Martin's arguments . . . that John C. Calhoun was wont to draw in his nullification speeches" (*Luther Martin: The "Federal Bull-Dog,"* 16). The editor of Calhoun's papers, Professor Clyde Wilson, tells me that although "Calhoun did not cite sources[,] I cannot remember a single specific mention of Luther Martin." Letter to the author, June 14, 2006.

33. Elliot, *Debates*, Vol. 3, 57.

34. Martin, "The Genuine Information," Farrand, *Records of the Federal Convention*, Vol. 3, 223.

35. "Letter from the Hon. Richard Henry Lee, Esq., to his Excellency, Edmund Randolph, Esq.," in Elliot, *Debates*, Vol. 1, 503.

36. Martin, "The Genuine Information," Farrand, *Records of the Federal Convention*, Vol. 3, 230–32.

37. Rutland, *The Ordeal of the Constitution*, 74.

38. "The Landholder, VIII," December 24, 1787, Farrand, *Records of the Federal Convention*, Vol. 3, 171.

39. "Luther Martin's Defense of Gerry," in ibid., 259.

40. "The Landholder, X," in ibid., 271–75. Although the February 29, 1788 "Landholder" letter has traditionally been credited to Oliver Ellsworth, John Kaminski and Gaspare J. Saladino speculate that it may have been written by Martin's nationalist Maryland colleague, Daniel of St. Thomas

Jenifer. John Kaminski and Gaspare J. Saladino, editors, *Documentary History of the Ratification of the Constitution*, Vol. 16 (Madison, WI: State Historical Society of Wisconsin, 1986), 265–66.

41. Quoted in William Garrott Brown, *The Life of Oliver Ellsworth* (New York: Macmillan, 1905), 5.

42. Martin, *Modern Gratitude*, 39–40.

43. Clarkson and Jett, *Luther Martin of Maryland*, 306.

44. "Luther Martin's Reply to the Landholder," March 14, 1788, Farrand, *Records of the Federal Convention*, Vol. 3, 281–86.

45. "Luther Martin's Reply to the Landholder," March 19, 1788, in ibid., 289.

46. Ibid., 292.

47. Elliot, *Debates*, Vol. 3, 48, 53–54.

48. Miner, *Our Rude Forefathers*, 204.

49. Martin, "The Genuine Information," Farrand, *Records of the Federal Convention*, Vol. 3, 221. At the Massachusetts ratifying convention, Samuel Adams proposed an amendment that delineated, in large measure, the eventual Bill of Rights: "And that the said Constitution be never construed to authorize Congress to infringe the just liberty of the press, or the rights of conscience; or to prevent the people of the United States, who are peaceable citizens, from keeping their own arms; or to raise standing armies, unless when necessary for the defence of the United States, or of some one or more of them; or to prevent the people from petitioning, in a peaceable and orderly manner, the federal legislature, for a redress of grievances; or to subject the people to unreasonable searches and seizures of their persons, papers or possessions." Harding, *The Contest Over Ratification of the Federal Constitution in the State of Massachusetts*, 98.

50. Martin, "The Genuine Information," Farrand, *Records of the Federal Convention*, Vol. 3, 211–12.

51. Ibid., 197.

52. Ibid., 210.

53. Elliot, *Debates*, Vol. 3, 452–53.

54. Ibid., 590.

55. William Frederick Poole, *Anti-Slavery Opinions Before 1800* (Cincinnati: Robert Clarke & Co., 1873), 50.

56. "Luther Martin's Reply to the Landholder," March 19, 1788, Farrand, *Records of the Federal Convention*, Vol. 3, 290–91.

57. Martin, "The Genuine Information," Farrand, *Records of the Federal Convention*, Vol. 3, 207.

58. Quoted in Jensen, *The Articles of Confederation*, 194.

59. Elliot, *Debates*, Vol. 2, 137.

60. Martin, "The Genuine Information," Farrand, *Records of the Federal Convention*, Vol. 3, 208.

61. Ibid., 209.

62. "Luther Martin's Reply to the Landholder," March 14, 1788, Farrand, *Records of the Federal Convention*, Vol. 3, 285.

63. Quoted in Clarkson and Jett, *Luther Martin of Maryland*, 191.

64. Elliot, *Debates*, Vol. 3, 485.

65. Elliot, *Debates*, Vol. 2, 287–88.

66. Martin, "The Genuine Information," Farrand, *Records of the Federal Convention*, Vol. 3, 194.

67. "Letter from the Hon. Robert Yates and the Hon. John Lansing, Jun., Esquires," Elliot, *Debates*, Vol. 1, 481.

68. Paine, *Common Sense*, 28.

69. Elliot, *Debates*, Vol. 3, 266–67.

70. "Philadelphiensis," February 7, 1788, in Kenyon, *The Antifederalists*, 72.

71. Elliot, *Debates*, Vol. 2, 249.

72. Madison, *Notes of Debates in the Federal Convention of 1787*, 263.

73. Elliot, *Debates*, Vol. 4, 51.

74. Elliot, *Debates*, Vol. 2, 419.

75. Luther Martin, "The Genuine Information," Farrand, *Records of the Federal Convention*, Vol. 3, 196.

76. Elliot, *Debates*, Vol. 3, 30–31.

77. Elliot, *Debates*, Vol. 2, 353.

78. James Madison, "Federalist No. 10," in Madison, Alexander Hamilton, and John Jay, *The Federalist Papers* (New York: New America, 1961 [1788]), 83–84.

79. James Madison, "Federalist No. 46," in ibid., 297.

80. Elliot, *Debates*, Vol. 2, 256–57.

81. Ibid., 262.

82. Ibid., 267.

83. Ibid., 305.

84. Ibid., 312.

85. Ibid., 376.

86. Storing, *What the Anti-Federalists Were* For, 7.

87. "Luther Martin's Reply to the Landholder," March 19, 1788, Farrand, *Records of the Federal Convention*, Vol. 3, 294.

88. Elliot, *Debates*, Vol. 3, 641.

89. Elliot, *Debates*, Vol. 2, 401–4.

90. Elliot, *Debates*, Vol. 3, 521.

91. Elliot, *Debates*, Vol. 4, 139.

92. Pierce Butler to Weedon Butler, May 5, 1788, Farrand, *Records of the Federal Convention*, Vol. 3, 302.

93. Rutland, *The Ordeal of the Constitution*, 95.

94. Elliot, *Debates*, Vol. 2, 246.

95. "Philadelphiensis," in Kenyon, *The Antifederalists*, 69–71.

96. "Luther Martin's Reply to the Landholder," March 19, 1788, Farrand, *Records of the Federal Convention*, Vol. 3, 291.

97. Quoted in Rutland, *The Ordeal of the Constitution*, 157.

98. James Madison to George Washington, April 10, 1788, in *The Writings of James Madison*, Vol. 5, edited by Gaillard Hunt (New York: Putnam's, 1904), 116–17.

99. Quoted in B. C. Steiner, "Maryland's Adoption of the Federal Constitution," *American Historical Review*, Vol. 5, No. 1 (October 1899): 36.

100. Elliot, *Debates*, Vol. 2, 547.

101. Ibid., 548–49.

102. Ibid., 550.

103. Ibid., 552–53.

104. Ibid., 555.

105. Crowl, "Anti-Federalism in Maryland, 1787–1788," *William and Mary Quarterly*: 469.

106. Tyler, *Memoir of Roger Brooke Taney*, 69–70.

107. George Washington to James Madison, May 2, 1788, in *The Papers of George Washington*, Vol. 6, edited by Dorothy Twohig (Charlottesville: University Press of Virginia, 1997), 258.

108. Bowen, *Miracle at Philadelphia*, 78.

109. Rutland, *The Ordeal of the Constitution*, 313.

110. Quoted in Rossiter, *1787: The Grand Convention*, 286.

111. Michael Lienesch, "North Carolina: Preserving Rights," in *Ratifying the Constitution*, edited by Michael Allen Gillespie and Michael Lienesch (Lawrence, KS: University Press of Kansas, 1989), 343.

112. Quoted in James T. Austin, *The Life of Elbridge Gerry* (Boston: Wells and Lilly, 1829), 67.

113. Elliot, *Debates*, Vol. 3, 605, 607.

114. Lienesch, "In Defence of the Antifederalists," *History of American Political Thought*: 85.

115. "Luther Martin's Reply to the Landholder," March 14, 1788, Farrand, *Records of the Federal Convention*, Vol. 3, 286.

116. Quoted in Haw et al., *Stormy Patriot: The Life of Samuel Chase*, 155, 164.

Part Three: Of Chase and Burr and Unmarked Graves

1. Tyler, *Memoir of Roger Brooke Taney*, 68.

2. Kenneth Bailey, *Thomas Cresap: Maryland Frontiersman* (Boston: Christopher Publishing House, 1944), 66, 174, 176.

3. Ibid., 64.

4. Luther Martin, "Mr. Martin's VIIIth Letter to the Philosopher Jefferson," Letter of February 26, 1798, *Porcupine's Gazette*, Maryland Historical Society Library.

5. Thomas Jefferson, *Notes on the State of Virginia*, in *Thomas Jefferson: Writings* (New York: Library of America, 1984 [1787]), 188–89.

6. Luther Martin, "To the Editor of the *Porcupine's Gazette*," Letter of March 30, 1797, Maryland Historical Society Library. Clarkson and Jett provide a thorough account of Martin's attempt to clear the Cresap name in *Luther Martin of Maryland*, 171–88. An appendix includes George Rogers Clark's letter to Jefferson exonerating Cresap.

7. Ibid.

8. Luther Martin, Letter of December 11, 1797, *Porcupine's Gazette*, Maryland Historical Society Library.

9. George Rogers Clark to Dr. Samuel Browne, June 17, 1798, in Clarkson and Jett, *Luther Martin of Maryland*, 308.

10. John Dos Passos, *The Men Who Made the Nation* (Garden City, NY: Doubleday, 1957), 359.

11. Martin, *Modern Gratitude*, 1.

12. Ibid., 15.

13. Ibid., 25.

14. Ibid., 49.

15. Ibid., 9.

16. Ibid., 14–15.

17. Ibid., 60.

18. Ibid., 52–53.

19. Ibid., 72.

20. Richard Raynal Keene, *Letter from Richard Raynal Keene to Luther Martin, Esq., Attorney-General of Maryland, Upon the Subject of His "Modern Gratitude"* (Baltimore: Prentiss & Cole, 1802), 42.

21. Martin, *Modern Gratitude*, 2.

22. Ibid., 35.

23. Ibid., 38.

24. Ibid., 120.

25. Ibid., 163.

26. Keene, *Letter from Richard Raynal Keene to Luther Martin, Esq.*, 4.

27. Robert F. Brent, "Luther Martin as a Lawyer and a Lover," *Report of the Fourth Annual Meeting of the Maryland State Bar Association*, edited by Conway W. Sams (Baltimore: Hanzsche & Co., 1899), 78–81.

28. Bradford, *Founding Fathers*, 112.

29. Goddard, *Luther Martin: The "Federal Bull-Dog,"* 37–38.

30. Obrecht, "The Influence of Luther Martin in the Making of the Constitution of the United States," *Maryland Historical Magazine*: 183.

31. Tyler, *Memoir of Roger Brooke Taney*, 66.

32. *The National Portrait Gallery of Distinguished Americans*, 6.

33. Joseph Story to Samuel P. Fay, *Life and Letters of Joseph Story*, Vol. 1, edited by William W. Story (Boston: Charles C. Little and James Brown, 1851), 163–64.

34. Tyler, *Memoir of Roger Brooke Taney*, 64–67.

35. Ibid., 69.

36. Ibid., 122–23.

37. Monroe Johnson, "Introducing 'Federal Bulldog,'" *National Republic* (Dec. 1934): 12–13.

38. Quoted in Clarkson and Jett, *Luther Martin of Maryland*, 190.

39. *Baltimore American*, April 11, 1801, Maryland Historical Society Library, Box 1751, Clarkson Letters.

40. Albert J. Beveridge, *The Life of John Marshall*, Vol. 3 (Boston: Houghton Mifflin, 1919), 186.

41. Quoted in Storing, *What the Anti-Federalists Were For*, 50.

42. Henry Adams, *John Randolph* (Boston: Houghton Mifflin, 1882), 134.

43. Beveridge, *The Life of John Marshall*, Vol. 3, 184.

44. Stephen B. Presser, "A Tale of Two Judges: Richard Peters, Samuel Chase, and the Broken Promise of Federalist Jurisprudence," *Northwestern University Law Review* 73 (March–April 1978): 72. For a reassessment of Justice Chase, see also Stephen B. Presser, *The Original Misunderstanding: The English, the Americans and the Dialectic of Federalist Jurisprudence* (Durham, NC: Carolina Academic Press, 1991).

45. Ibid.: 92.

46. Quoted in Haw et al., *Stormy Patriot: The Life of Samuel Chase,* 198.

47. Quoted in Presser, "A Tale of Two Judges: Richard Peters, Samuel Chase, and the Broken Promise of Federalist Jurisprudence," *Northwestern University Law Review*: 97.

48. Quoted in Raoul Berger, *Impeachment: The Constitutional Problems* (Cambridge: Harvard University Press, 1973), 233.

49. Presser, "A Tale of Two Judges: Richard Peters, Samuel Chase, and the Broken Promise of Federalist Jurisprudence," *Northwestern University Law Review*: 99.

50. Quoted in Haw et al., *Stormy Patriot: The Life of Samuel Chase,* 215.

51. Thomas Jefferson to Joseph Nicholson, May 13, 1803, *The Jefferson Cyclopedia*, 135.

52. Quoted in Haw et al., *Stormy Patriot: The Life of Samuel Chase,* 222.

53. "Letter from the Hon. Richard Henry Lee, Esq., to His Excellency Edmund Randolph, Esq.," Elliot, *Debates*, Vol. 1, 503.

54. Madison, *Notes of Debates in the Federal Convention of 1787*, 314.

55. "Luther Martin Before the Maryland House of Representatives," November 29, 1787, Farrand, *Records of the Federal Convention*, Vol. 3, 152.

56. Joseph Hopkinson, "Hail Columbia," in *The Poets and Poetry of America*,

edited by Rufus Wilmot Griswold (Philadelphia: Parry and McMillan, 1858), 72.

57. Adams, *John Randolph*, 138.

58. For a legal scholar's brief that Chase's impeachment was "richly justified" (251) and that his "removal from office would have served as a standing reminder that there is no room on our bench for an implacably prejudiced judge" (224), see Berger, *Impeachment: The Constitutional Problems.*

59. Beveridge, *The Life of John Marshall*, Vol. 3, 157.

60. Ibid., 205.

61. William Plumer, *William Plumer's Memorandum of Proceedings in the United States Senate: 1803–1807*, edited by Everett Somerville Brown (New York: Macmillan, 1923), 300.

62. Quoted in Beveridge, *The Life of John Marshall*, Vol. 3, 214.

63. Rehnquist, *Grand Inquests: The Historic Impeachments of Justice Samuel Chase and President Andrew Johnson*, 103.

64. Ibid., 114.

65. Adams, *John Randolph*, 141.

66. Ibid., 143, 147.

67. Quoted in Goddard, *Luther Martin: The "Federal Bull-Dog,"* 22.

68. Clarkson and Jett, *Luther Martin of Maryland*, 280.

69. Quoted in Goddard, *Luther Martin: The "Federal Bull-Dog,"* 30.

70. Nathan Schachner, *Aaron Burr: A Biography* (New York: Perpetua, 1961 [1937]), 15.

71. Vidal, *Burr*, 2–3.

72. Charles A. Beard, "Introduction," in Walter F. McCaleb, *The Aaron Burr Conspiracy* (New York: Argosy-Antiquarian, 1966 [1903, 1936]), x.

73. Wood, *Revolutionary Characters: What Made the Founders Different*, 234.

74. Henry Adams, *History of the United States During the Second Administration of Thomas Jefferson*, Vol. 1 (New York: Scribner's, 1909), 298.

75. Ibid., 226.

76. Quoted in Buckner F. Melton, Jr., *Aaron Burr: Conspiracy to Treason* (New York: Wiley, 2002), 54.

77. Ibid., 235.

78. Adams, *History of the United States During the Second Administration of Thomas Jefferson*, Vol. 1, 255.

79. William H. Safford, *The Life of Harman Blennerhassett* (Cincinnati: Moore, Anderson, Wilstach & Keys, 1853), 66.

80. Quoted in Schachner, *Aaron Burr: A Biography*, 511.

81. Adams, *History of the United States During the Second Administration of Thomas Jefferson*, Vol. 1, 234.

82. Beveridge, *The Life of John Marshall*, Vol. 3, 324–25.

83. Ibid., 390.

84. Goddard, *Luther Martin: The "Federal Bull-Dog,"* 24.

85. Schachner, *Aaron Burr: A Biography*, 416.

86. Quoted in Goddard, *Luther Martin: The "Federal Bull-Dog,"* 25.

87. Quoted in Beveridge, *The Life of John Marshall*, Vol. 3, 436.

88. Quoted in Adams, *History of the United States During the Second Administration of Thomas Jefferson*, Vol. 1, 449.

89. Thomas Jefferson to George Hay, June 19, 1807, *The Jefferson Cyclopedia*, 542.

90. Quoted in Joseph Wheelan, *Jefferson's Vendetta: The Pursuit of Aaron Burr and the Judiciary* (New York: Carroll & Graf, 2005), 254.

91. Schachner, *Aaron Burr: A Biography*, 131. Clarkson and Jett, *Luther Martin of Maryland*, 254.

92. Adams, *History of the United States During the Second Administration of Thomas Jefferson*, Vol. 1, 465.

93. Quoted in Wheelan, *Jefferson's Vendetta: The Pursuit of Aaron Burr and the Judiciary*, 169.

94. Quoted in Beveridge, *The Life of John Marshall*, Vol. 3, 506.

95. Rehnquist, *Grand Inquests: The Historic Impeachments of Justice Samuel Chase and President Andrew Johnson,* 118.

96. Quoted in Melton, *Aaron Burr: Conspiracy to Treason*, 218.

97. Safford, *The Life of Harman Blennerhassett,* 170–72.

98. *Harman Blennerhassett's Journal, 1807*, edited by Raymond E. Fitch (Athens, OH: Ohio University Press, 1988), 132, 141.

99. Ibid., 108.

100. Quoted in Brent, "Luther Martin as a Lawyer and a Lover," *Report of the Fourth Annual Meeting of the Maryland State Bar Association*: 83.

101. Quoted in Clarkson and Jett, *Luther Martin of Maryland*, 264.

102. *The Scourge* (Baltimore), September 22, 1810, Vol. 1, No. 17, 1–2, Maryland Historical Society Library, Box 1751, Clarkson Letters.

103. Clarkson and Jett provide the only mention I have seen of Juliet (*Luther Martin of Maryland*, 57). Yet in *Modern Gratitude* (15), Martin writes, "I was the father of two daughters."

104. Luther Martin to Dr. Thomas Parke, May 20, 1815, Maryland Historical Society Library, Box 1751, Clarkson Letters.

105. Luther Martin to Dr. Thomas Parke, July 1, 1815, in ibid.

106. Luther Martin to Dr. Thomas Parke, January 14, 1816, in ibid.

107. Goddard, *Luther Martin: The "Federal Bull-Dog,"* 35.

108. Joseph Story to Nathaniel Williams, February 16, 1812, in *Life and Letters of Joseph Story*, 214.

109. *McCulloch v. The State of Maryland et al.*, in Henry Wheaton, *Reports of cases argued and adjudged in the Supreme Court of the United States* (Philadelphia: Matthew Carey, 1816–1827), Vol. 4, 372–73.

110. Quoted in Beveridge, *The Life of John Marshall*, Vol. 4, 294.

111. Quoted in ibid., 295–96.

112. Quoted in Leonard W. Levy, *Seasoned Judgments: The American Constitution, Rights, and History* (New Brunswick, NJ: Transaction, 1995), 427.

113. Ibid., 429.

114. Quoted in ibid., 424.

115. Tyler, *Memoir of Roger Brooke Taney*, 142.

116. Goddard, *Luther Martin: The "Federal Bull-Dog,"* 10–11.

117. Quoted in Tyler, *Memoir of Roger Brooke Taney*, 142.

118. Martin, *Modern Gratitude*, 36.

119. Quoted in Goddard, *Luther Martin: The "Federal Bull-Dog,"* 31.

120. Tyler, *Memoir of Roger Brooke Taney*, 69.

121. Goddard, *Luther Martin: The "Federal Bull-Dog,"* 11.

122. "Honorable Luther Martin, of Maryland," Resolution of the Bench and Bar of Baltimore, Maryland Historical Society Library, Pamphlet 11508.

123. Martin, "The Genuine Information," Farrand, *Records of the Federal Convention*, Vol. 3, 190.

INDEX

ALSO BY BILL KAUFFMAN

Ain't My America
America First!
Country Towns of New York
Dispatches from the Muckdog Gazette
Every Man a King
Look Homeward, America
With Good Intentions?
Bye Bye, Miss American Empire
Copperhead: A Screenplay
Poetry Night at the Ballpark and Other Scenes from an Alternative America

INTERCOLLEGIATE
STUDIES INSTITUTE
Educating for Liberty

ISI Books is the publishing imprint of the **Intercollegiate Studies Institute**, whose mission is to inspire college students to discover, embrace, and advance the principles and virtues that make America free and prosperous.

Founded in 1953, ISI teaches future leaders the core ideas behind the free market, the American Founding, and Western civilization that are rarely taught in the classroom.

ISI is a nonprofit, nonpartisan, tax-exempt educational organization. The Institute relies on the financial support of the general public—individuals, foundations, and corporations—and receives no funding or any other aid from any level of the government.

www.isi.org